Crossing the Congo

Mike Martin, Chloe Baker,
Charlie Hatch-Barnwell

Crossing the Congo

Over Land and Water in a Hard Place

HURST & COMPANY, LONDON

First published in the United Kingdom in 2016 by
C. Hurst & Co. (Publishers) Ltd.,
41 Great Russell Street, London, WC1B 3PL
© Mike Martin, Chloe Baker and Charlie Hatch-Barnwell, 2016
All rights reserved.
All photographs © Charlie Hatch-Barnwell

Distributed in the United States, Canada and Latin America by
Oxford University Press, 198 Madison Avenue, New York, NY 10016,
United States of America.

The rights of Mike Martin, Chloe Baker and Charlie Hatch-Barnwell to be identified as
the authors of this publication is asserted by them in accordance with the Copyright,
Designs and Patents Act, 1988.

A Cataloguing-in-Publication data record for this book is available from the British
Library.

This book is printed using paper from registered sustainable and managed sources.

9781849046855   *cloth*

www.hurstpublishers.com

www.crossingthecongo.com

Printed and bound by Bell and Bain Ltd, Glasgow

Contents

Preface

People constantly complain that there is nothing left to explore in the world: no challenges left on this planet's surface. We must look to the bottom of the oceans, to canopies or caves, or to other worlds to rediscover the pioneering and exploring spirit shown by history's great explorers.

I believe, however, that this overlooks the fact that often the main landscape being mapped by explorers is the internal one. When the tiredness, the grumpiness, the weakness sets in—as it must on any long, independent journey—how do these people respond? The most interesting answer is not whether they succeed or fail in their endeavour to complete whatever challenge they have set themselves, or how they set about solving the challenges that they face (although these are both worthy aspects of a journey). It is how groups of people navigate their group dynamics, their internal landscapes, and how it changes them, their composure and their self-image. This outstanding book seeks to understand all these three aspects of exploration.

This team were certainly not the first to cross the Congo river basin; but it had been sufficiently long since their particular route had been completed that it was largely lost to the elements; it was tough, unknown and required ingenuity. Even recently, others have crossed parts of the Congo using alternative modes of transport and different routes, but none of them has crossed the broad sweep of the country independently. And what of their internal challenge? As they put it themselves, 'we had got through, but we had lost our dignity, our composure, our "civilisation"'.

Hearing of their expedition reminded me of my own crossing of the Amazon basin in 1958. That journey was longer, and less technology was available; and crocodiles, piranhas and bandits were a concern. But the Congo in 2013 was recently post-conflict and highly volatile, requiring a degree of political nous not required by Richard and me in the 1950s. Nor did we have to deal with appallingly kleptocratic officials, desperate to keep the team out of certain areas lest they discover their criminal secrets. Different times, different external challenges, but the same internal landscape of discovery.

Crossing the Congo gives you a deeply, brutally honest view of what it is like to complete a great journey. At times they were lucky to survive.

Robin Hanbury-Tenison OBE, FRGS • Bodmin, June 2015

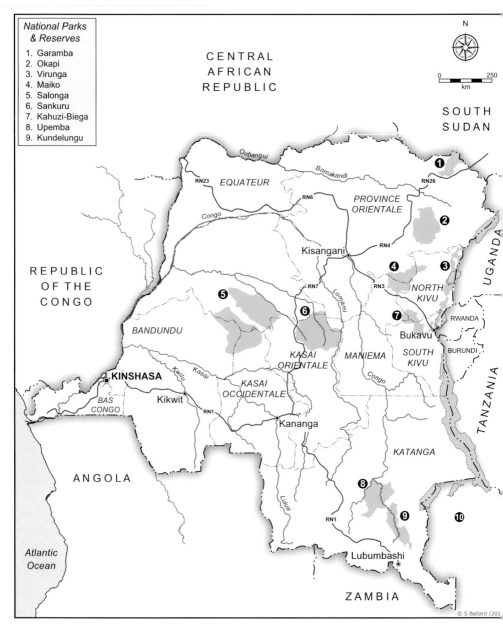

Democractic Republic of Cong

Introduction Chloe Baker

Driving across the Congo was not something any of us ever expected to do. But in just two short months we had travelled further than we could ever have imagined. In many ways the three of us went on different journeys, all held together by three dominant themes. The first, an incredible and at times ridiculous adventure that forms the substrate of the book—an intensely physical journey across phenomenal terrain. The second, an introduction to a brutalised people, the Congolese. And the third, a journey through our own group dynamic, our emotions and behaviours, changing forever our assumptions about humanity, and our own self-perceptions.

These themes are complementary and interweave throughout our story, and this book. Nothing turned out as we had expected. The first thread is clearly defined and concluded, the second merely an introduction. The brutalisation of the Congo, by its own people and by others, continues; we only scratched the surface in our time there. And the last theme is perhaps the least conclusive of all. The Congo marked a rupture in our personal lives, but the experience of vulnerability, frustration and anger, and of reason and civilisation slipping through our fingers, has started for each of us an ongoing journey, hopefully towards a new understanding of ourselves.

Four months earlier, Mike and I had set off from England during the snowy February of 2013 in a 1986 Land Rover 90. Our car was called 9Bob because, as he'd rolled off a repair truck onto my mum's drive, we'd realised that the man who'd sold him to us was bent as a nine bob note (British slang for shady). We'd bought the car online and Mike had hastily finished its conversion from right- to left-hand drive using the infamous Haynes Manual (a sort of how-to guide for the uninitiated [Haynes 2015]), advice from passing neighbours and postmen, and the wealth of information on online Land Rover forums.

The learning curve had been steep, and the work miserable: twisting, banging and occasionally snapping rusty nuts under the car in the dark, cold, wet December evenings. Mike had started the process knowing nothing about mechanics—indeed, had he known more, he may have been wise enough never to embark on the project. That autumn, he had also written and submitted his PhD thesis about the conflict in Afghanistan. I had taken my first set of professional anaesthetics exams between hectic A&E shifts as a junior doctor in East London, where we lived together, engaged to be married.

We had left the UK with the intention of driving as far around West Africa as time would allow us, and then heading home via Europe before my new job started in August. We hoped to improve our French as well as scoping out possible cities where we would be happy to work together in the future. As conflicts began to erupt across northern Africa, in Algeria, Mali and the Central African Republic, our options for making a circular trip became progressively more limited, and while staying with some nuns in Ouagadougou, Burkina Faso, we began to explore the option of heading home via the Democratic Republic of Congo (DRC), South Sudan, Sudan and Egypt.

Internet searches told us how difficult, if not impossible, this would be. A Belgian couple had driven across the southern part of the DRC in 2010, regularly having to right their Land Cruiser after it toppled onto its side, or winch it out of muddy predicaments (Frederik and Josephine 2010). Some intrepid canoeists had ventured across the country retracing Stanley's epic attempts to follow the River Congo to its source (Tayler 2001; Harwood 2013), and a couple of brave motorcyclists and hitchhikers had managed to cross the country using the large barges (basically floating markets) that ply the River Congo between Kinshasa, the capital of the DRC, and Kisangani, the country's third largest city.

Best of all, in 2011, one courageous Estonian man and his Portuguese friend had driven some of a route in the north-east of the country between the South Sudanese border and Kisangani in a Mazda minivan. They had had to turn back after being rescued from one too many muddy holes by the UN (Tarmo 2011). This Estonian man, and his very funny blog, became a source of inspiration for Mike as we got closer to the Congo. As far as we were aware, only one other man had tried the north-east route—managing to travel between Juba and Kisangani by public transport (Frankonia 2012).

The titles alone of the books written about the DRC are enough to deter any reasonable person: *Facing the Congo: A Modern-Day Journey into the Heart of Darkness* (Tayler 2001), or *Blood River: The Terrifying Journey Through the World's Most Dangerous Country* (Butcher 2009). Besides describing the atrocious quality of the roads, the books and reports were also united in their horror at the corrupt and wild officials of the country. From what we read, it seemed the DRC was teeming with often drunk and stoned police, military and other figures who would resort to violent enforcement of their will at the slightest provocation. A recently updated guidebook to the Congos did little to dispel the prejudice—recommending greeting any police officer with a banknote in your palm (Rorison 2012).

During the earlier parts of this trip, and during time living and working in other fragile areas, Mike and I had learnt to unpick some of this rhetoric. Undoubtedly these challenges would face us, but we were also both strong believers in innate goodness, convinced that with time it was usually possible to find common ground with most people.

All of this was probably irrelevant, though, since our internet research also told us that it is extremely challenging to get a visa for the DRC without letters of invitation, and impossible to apply for one outside your country of residence. We were a long, long way from home and could not risk posting our passports back. We had already been refused a Gabon visa at the embassy in Abidjan simply because they didn't like our choice of shoes, and we were well aware of the unpredictable and apparently illogical processes employed by embassies of many countries in the region as part of what we interpreted as a principle of 'reciprocity'. As far as we could tell, this boiled down to a kind of guerrilla justice whereby embassies endeavour to show Europeans and Americans how they too can make it difficult to get a visa—a dose of our own medicine if you like. Apparently, the DRC had perfected this craft.

Furthermore, there were also numerous stories in overland travel blogs about people arriving at the border of the DRC with everything in order, and still being refused entry for a multitude of spurious reasons. I didn't go to the DRC against my will exactly, but I was a lot less enthusiastic than Mike. I was genuinely concerned that we might die or get seriously hurt, accidentally or otherwise, and although a bit of me wanted to go, I was definitely apprehensive. Fine, I thought, I'll risk letting Mike go to an embassy so that he can get it out of his system. We agreed to try and get a visa in a couple of countries along our route, but if all failed we'd turn around and go home the way we came, snaking back through Senegal and Mauritania.

The embassy in Cotonou, Benin, was our first attempt. We would be there a while anyway, while Mike replaced the clutch, inside which a crucial part had sheared off. Visas always took a while. If we failed there, we would try Lomé, Togo, where they allowed 'overlanders' to buy a week's temporary residence to bypass the Congolese visa rule. As it turned out, the embassy of the DRC in Cotonou is staffed by some of the most affable gentlemen we would ever meet. Still, we felt uncomfortable handing over our money and passports—we'd read many reports of the latter alone being returned, along with a letter of refusal.

Our concerns were utterly misplaced. Not only did they issue our visas within forty-eight hours—the epitome of efficiency—but the chargé d'affaires also lent us the use of his car and driver to go to the airport and tackle the complicated customs process for our imported clutch (which Charlie had couriered to us at vast cost). The next couple of days would find Honoré, the driver, alongside Mike working under the car in a church compound, using an improvised pulley system to hang the gearbox from the roof of the car in order to change the clutch. His help was invaluable. Sadly we didn't get to thank him properly. He didn't turn up for the dinner we'd offered to buy him, presumably still disappointed by our conversation earlier in the day when he'd asked us to find him a job in the UK as a driver.

It pained us not to be able to help Honoré and the legion of other respectable, hard-working and honest people who were to ask the same of us daily during our journey. It was deeply unfair that we could pass through the region at liberty, receiving their warmth and hospitality, and yet could not reciprocate. My experience visiting detention centres in the UK, where I had worked with asylum seekers and economic migrants as a doctor, and Mike's knowledge of London's Afghan diaspora, told us that someone trying to migrate from a relatively comfortable position—as in Honoré's case—would have dismal prospects of making it into the UK legally. The people we met all shared the same dream, a dream of reaching Europe, where they felt hard work would translate into a safe and secure future for their families. We were witness to the groundswell of desire to get to Europe that has tragically led to many African migrants drowning while trying to cross the Mediterranean from 2014 onwards.

An Idea Becoming a Reality

We touched up 9Bob's paintwork, and packed our tools, leaving Cotonou. Heading towards the Nigerian border, it dawned on us that crossing the Congo might be a reality.

We had already covered some pretty challenging terrain in Guinea and Liberia, and were reasonably confident of the car's capabilities and our driving skills. We also seemed to have encountered most possible breakdown situations that the car could invent, and Mike had thought or hammered our way out of them all—including a snow blizzard in the Pyrenees, the blazing desert sun in Mauritania and the sodden rainforest of Cameroon. We had also had some taxing interactions with military, customs and police officials, particularly in Cote d'Ivoire and Nigeria, and had not yet paid a single bribe, so perhaps we thought we could manage that aspect too. There had been many inspiring acts of kindness from the people we'd met and we were hopeful that our luck would hold.

Despite all of this, we knew we were woefully ill-prepared for a journey that most sensible people would spend at least twelve months setting up. We got on the internet at every major city and searched for more information on blogs and the like, but with little success. Mike excitedly pored over the maps that we'd brought along just in case, and we ordered a 'guidebook' to supplement them. We combed garages in relatively affluent Nigeria and Cameroon for spare parts and various oils, and again ordered more online. We sought the other necessary visas: the Republic of Congo and South Sudan.

The most important thing that we did, however, was to recruit Charlie to our adventure. Mike and Charlie had been friends since they were seven, and Charlie now splits his time between managing an award-winning kebab shop in West London, running an educational charity in Indonesia, and being an intrepid photojournalist. Between trips to Indonesia and Tanzania he checked his emails and was immediately hooked. The two of them had travelled across Southeast Asia and South America previously and both were keen to relive the dream. We needed Charlie for morale and creativity as well as for another pair of hands on deck, and the security of having another man present. We also needed him to bring to the DRC all of the replacement parts we had ordered online, including a spare fuel tank (our previous one had been leaking since Sierra Leone).

We have often been questioned about our motivations since returning. Why did you do it? It is a good question. The answer is still not immediately obvious. We mutter platitudes about it being a life experience, a good challenge. It was; but it was also at times deeply unpleasant. There was an element of necessity—it was the best solution to getting home that we could devise. But there was more to it than that. It was the uniqueness and the opportunity. Not many people do things like that. Discovery is another important word. Not just discovery of a little-known land, but an exploration of our personal limits and the depths of our convictions. This trip brought to the surface aspects of our personalities we were not proud of. It was also about complete freedom, to sink or swim on our own merits. That is a freedom that you don't often get in the safety of our modern world.

The largest part of it, though, was that people said that it could not be done. That it was impossible.

Entering the DRC

Things started to go wrong almost immediately when we visited the bustling port in Brazzaville, Republic of Congo (ROC), to buy boat tickets to Kinshasa for the next day. A harassed and busy porter welcomed us by accidentally dropping a box of frozen fish onto my head. We then found out that the car loading mechanism on the barge was broken. Instead of forty-five minutes, our journey to Kinshasa, standing in full view across the river, would take the best part of two days. In retrospect, we should have seen this as an omen. That night Mike and I had another conversation in a long series about whether we should continue with our plans to get married.

Leaving the ROC entailed the usual challenges of unconstructed roads, sparse navigational clues and confused officials, but was otherwise uncomplicated. We found ourselves being stamped out of the country not long after lunchtime the next day. Here began the most surreal border crossing yet. Leaving the isolated customs and immigration hut behind, we passed several large concrete block signs indicating our entry into 'Congo Belge' (the other side welcomed one to 'Congo Français'). No-one, it seemed, had thought to remove them in the fifty-three years since independence. We were always a little uneasy in the no-man's land between countries and were fearful of missing the immigration post as we had between Senegal and Guinea, without which we could not enter the new country legally.

This no-man's land was particularly bizarre. As we followed the unpaved road through rolling mountains it gradually branched into smaller tracks. We tried to maintain as straight a line as possible, hoping not to miss the crossing point and end up in trouble. All we could see around us were tree-covered mountains dotted with areas of bare rock face and boulders. We knew we were headed for a place called Mani Yanga, but it was not marked on our map and we had no grid references. Several times we had to turn around or back up, as the tracks cracked into 9Bob-sized ravines, or the camber of the mountain side threatened to send us into a roll. Once or twice we saw a man or two on the track, but they would run away as soon as they spotted us in the distance.

Descending from a crest, we eventually encountered a padlocked bar across the track. There were no signs, but this could be it. The moment of truth—would they let us in? In fact, a more pertinent question was who would let us in? We were still in the middle of nowhere. Then, 200 yards down the cliff to our left we saw people moving around some huts. A man appeared out of a bush by the gate and indicated that we should honk our horn. They began the slow climb up the hill.

When they finally arrived we could see they were a crowd of twelve young men in flip flops, t-shirts and jeans. Before unlocking the padlocked gate they performed the most professional and thorough search of the car we had thus far encountered and welcomed us to the DRC. Mike walked with them down to the village while I drove behind. At the hut, Mike supervised the interrogation of the passports and answered questions, and I sat outside with some other 'officials' who politely asked about our plans. They seemed to find our arrival completely natural, though the blogger-sphere and a sly glance

at their ledger told us we were one of only three foreign cars to pass through in the last two years.

We left the village with a stoned 'immigration officer' loaded into our front seat. He was opportunistically hitching a lift home since it could be another week before any traffic came through the post. We still hadn't achieved a stamp in our passport, but we also hadn't yet been asked for a bribe or intimidated in any way. We began to be hopeful that the DRC wasn't as scary as we had feared.

These hopes were reinforced later that evening. The road to Luozi, the official customs post and alternative crossing point for the River Congo, was slow going—crumbling into sheer drop-offs and hair-raising crevices which often had to be traversed. We didn't arrive there until nightfall. The barge was finished for the day, but we were rapidly directed to the Catholic mission, whose staff let us erect our mosquito dome in their goat pen free of charge, and we enjoyed a quiet beer in the town's only bar. With the exception of the money-changing man, who seemed to think we were unable to count, everyone we met spoke good French and was open-faced, honest and mostly uninterested in us—a welcome relief.

The next day we began early on the journey to Kinshasa in order to meet Charlie's flight. In the event, he beat us by six hours, but had to remain in the airport: his options for entertainment were limited by the sixty-litre fuel tank he was carrying for us. The inevitable delays began first thing. Customs in Luozi had inexplicably lost their stamp, necessitating a later series of visits to various ports in Kinshasa in order to legally import our car into the country. Immigration did have a stamp, which they finally applied to our passports, despite our refusal to pay their additional $10. We made it to the port in time to be the third vehicle in the queue, meaning we would be on the first barge that morning. Unfortunately, a lorry driver arriving after us took exception to us being allowed on before him and began to shout accusations while poking Mike in the chest. He had been driving all night with the aid of stimulant drugs, which is not uncommon in the region. The pontoon's police officer and a passing soldier rapidly sprang to our defence, professionally defusing the situation and maintaining order.

On the other side of the river we drove for some time before reaching a road. On the way we passed streams of women in t-shirts and colourful wraps, with baskets of cassava and other root vegetables piled high on their heads, heading to a weekly market. The road was worth the wait. The smooth tarmac was some of the best we'd seen, and we sped towards Kinshasa. Very few police tried to stop us on the way, and not one asked for a bribe. One even stopped to salute us and then gestured for us to continue. We were passing through Bas Congo, one of the most prosperous and educated districts in the DRC, and relatively unscathed by the interminable conflicts elsewhere in the Congo.

The road deteriorated significantly as we entered Kinshasa, but the harassed traffic police, standing precariously amongst the potholes, worked valiantly to control the masses of vehicles. We stopped often to ask them directions to the airport, and though they couldn't help not one of them asked us for anything. Again, we started to question what we'd read about the DRC.

What you can read about the DRC

Everyone has heard of the DRC, and most people we know could find it on a map. The majority seem to associate it with jungle, violence, rape, rebels, child soldiers and minerals. For others, Ebola springs to mind, or the long civil war, one of the most lethal conflicts of all time. We all approached the trip with our own preconceptions. It had long been on my radar as a French-speaking, conflict-torn country in which to work as a doctor in the future. Mike was fascinated by the complex ethnic and tribal interactions intertwined with external interference, which had spawned an enduring internationalised civil war. It was not dissimilar to the situation in Afghanistan, where Mike had both fought and researched. Charlie saw adventure and the opportunity to take beautiful photos. For us all, the country held a certain romance.

The reality is not romantic. Throughout the DRC there is relentless poverty, and little palpable sense of hope for the future. The most recent UN report on the progress of the DRC admits that though significant advances have been made in democracy and economic growth in the country over recent years, it remains plagued by instability which prevents lasting development (RNDH 2014). According to this report, the causes of the instability lie among intercommunity rivalries, frequent waves of armed conflict in the east of the country, interference by its neighbours and the resulting chronic human rights violations including sexual violence. Government forces (usually rebranded militias), it reports, are not sufficient to control these problems or the country's borders, and those responsible for the chronic humanitarian crises and recurrent human rights violations enjoy impunity. This explains why, despite its impressive natural resources, the DRC remains 186th of 187 countries in the Human Development Report, with 84 per cent of the population suffering underemployment and up to two-thirds living below the poverty threshold. It is beyond comparison.

In order to better understand the current state of affairs in the DRC it is necessary to look to its modern history. To those readers who wish to know more than the brief summary below, I point them to the Belgian writer David Van Reybrouck. His excellent account of the recent political and social history of the DRC gives the Congolese a rare voice in their own history through a wide variety of in-depth interviews (Reybrouck 2014).

The current borders of the DRC were first established in 1884 when King Leopold II of Belgium used information provided by the Welsh explorer Sir Henry Morton Stanley to sketch out the Congo Free State—a country that Leopold would never visit himself. At the 1885 Conference of Berlin, where European powers divided up the African continent, Leopold formally declared the establishment of the country. It remained his personal property for the next twenty years. By the time Stanley arrived in 1876, the tribes of the Congo basin had long been suffering the ravages of Portuguese and African-Arab slave traders and ivory hunters. Things were not about to improve with the formation of the Congo Free State.

Though Leopold and Stanley worked hard to defeat the Muslim slave traders dominant in the region, the fate of the 'freed' slaves was little better. They were sent to isolated farms to gain a Christian missionary education as part of Leopold's quest to create the *mondele ndombe*—Christianised 'black white men'—and then compelled to enter the Free State's army: *la Force Publique*. (The word *mondele*—white man in Lingala—was later to follow us, as we were summoned, addressed and taunted with it as we drove across the country.) Meanwhile the Congolese endured a brutal regime of forced labour on rubber plantations. Whole villages were forcibly recruited, their work supervised by the *Force Publique* and discipline dispensed with the *chicotte* (a sharp-edged whip made from dried hippopotamus skin), hand amputation by machete, and summary execution. It is estimated that between five and ten million people died prematurely during the twenty years of Leopold's rule.

When the atrocities taking place in the Congo could no longer be ignored, the Belgian parliament forced Leopold to hand the country over, annexing it as a Belgian colony in 1908. They ruled along the principles of the *trinité coloniale*: state, missionary and corporate interests. Labour conditions improved very little, with mortality rates in rainforest labour camps of 20 per cent. To control the population a new form of 'scientific colonisation' emerged, with medical passports required for movement beyond the region of birth. Amazingly, travel restrictions still exist today, but without the medical passports—it is very hard to travel in the Congo if you are Congolese.

Belgian ethnographers also defined tribal identities, fixing them and teaching them in missionary schools described by Van Reybrouck as 'factories for tribal prejudice'. The compulsory schools provided a very basic primary education only, since no Congolese were ever destined for administrative posts. Although the Congo was to achieve one of the highest rates of literacy in Africa under Belgian rule, by the time it gained its independence in 1960 the country only had sixteen college graduates and not a single medical doctor. Meanwhile, under the Belgians, Congolese soldiers of the *Force Publique* fought in both the First and Second World Wars.

The Congolese resisted with counter-culture, music and religion. The most notable is Kimbanguism, an Africanised Christianity developed by the prophet-like miracle performer Simon Kimbangu. It retains some three million followers today. Imprisoned by the Belgians in 1921, he died in jail in 1951, and more than 100,000 of his followers were deported in cattle-trucks to rainforest labour camps. Despite this (or perhaps because of it) riots and protests sprang up around the country, and in 1960 the Belgians sketched a hasty route to Congolese independence. With little planning or preparation, the Republic of the Congo was unceremoniously announced. Unfortunately, and in an example of just how careless these flavours of colonialism were, the neighbouring French colony had also adopted the same name upon independence (which it keeps to the present day). The Congo Free State therefore become known as Congo-Léopoldville.

Patrice Lumumba, a former beer salesman from Stanleyville (now named Kisangani), became the country's first prime minister. Charismatic and idealistic, he articulated the national desire for freedom. Lumumba, although an inspirational speaker and visionary, was not an astute tactician, and did not hold back from publically denouncing colonial rule at the Independence Day ceremony on 30 June 1960. His lack of reserve injured Belgian pride, and in the context of emerging autonomy across the continent did little to allay American fears over access to Congolese uranium. The speech was to pave the way for his untimely end.

Relations with the Belgians rapidly deteriorated following independence, and when they began shelling the strategic port town of Matadi, Lumumba appealed to the UN for assistance. He also needed its support in the mineral-rich states of Katanga and Kasai, both of which announced their secession in late 1960. Help was not forthcoming, and Lumumba turned to the Soviets for support. In response, US President Eisenhower authorised his assassination by the CIA. A series of coups followed and although Lumumba temporarily gained UN protection, he was soon captured by rebels and transported to Élisabethville in the south of the country (now Lubumbashi). There he was beaten publicly and forced to eat copies of his own speeches before being shot dead. Four Belgians also took part in his murder.

Joseph-Désiré Mobutu, formerly Lumumba's closest ally and secretary and later his army chief of staff, was chosen by the Americans as his successor. The CIA facilitated the coup, paid the salaries of his allies and, along with the UN, aided him in defeating the Katangan secession in the south-east—support they had denied Lumumba. By 1965 Mobutu had declared himself president and was to rule for the next thirty-two years. His new name became *Mobutu Sese Seko Kuku Ngbendu Wa Za Banga*: 'the powerful warrior whose stamina and willpower carry him from victory to victory, leaving behind only fire'. In 1971 he renamed the country Zaire, and with the support of his western allies maintained oppressive, iron-fisted control. He used his security services and the single political party, the Mouvement Populaire de la Révolution (satirised as MPR, 'mourir pour rien'—the Congolese are linguistic geniuses), to spy on his friends and enemies alike.

Though history remembers Mobutu as the leopard-skin hat-adorned, vain, voluptuary dictator that he later became, he initially had high ideals. He aimed to re-Africanise Zaire, promoting a vibrant cultural revolution. He also launched a series of large-scale infrastructure projects, nationalised the mines and tackled ethnic and tribal divisions in the army and administration. Moving away from French, he used three major African languages—Lingala, Swahili and Tshiluba—to draw people together across tribal or ethnic boundaries. Through this and his 'authenticity' programme he was credited with creating a new and abiding sense of national identity.

Other legacies also remain. The DRC was the second most industrialised country in Africa at independence, but today it is one of the poorest. Mobutu's project of 'Zairianisation' saw the expropriation of all small businesses, farms and factories that belonged to the remaining foreigners in the country. With little experience running such enterprises, Zairians were unable to keep them afloat and the majority began to collapse, with stock sold and not replaced, and machinery left unrepaired and rusting. At the time that Mobutu was rumoured to be the seventh richest man in the world, Belgian roads and railways crumbled, and with little investment in the country it rapidly became dependent on imports. Inflation rose from 8 per cent in 1970 to 80 per cent in 1976 and to 101 per cent by 1979, partly as a consequence of rising oil prices. Food prices shot up and borrowing became necessary to pay off older debts. With the collapse of copper prices in the same decade, Mobutu finally had to change his economic plan.

Unable to pay state employees, Mobutu encouraged his citizens to steal in order to survive—telling them 'steal cleverly, little by little'. He advised people not to steal so much as to become rich overnight, otherwise one would be caught. Gradually stealing became a way of life, and 'fend for yourself' became an unofficial national motto. Mobutu amassed a personal fortune of between $1 billion and $5 billion, diverting foreign aid and investment to his own funds, and he supported those around him who did the same. Corruption became institutionalised. Officials embezzled soldiers' salaries and sold off arms for their own profit; the army stole truckloads of cobalt from the mines they were tasked to guard (it is estimated that over 10 per cent of metal produced by nationalised mines was stolen); postal workers stole expatriates' *Time* and *Newsweek* magazines in order to sell them on the black market. *Le mal zaïrois* (Zairean sickness)—a term coined by Mobutu himself—became engrained in the national psyche.

Although the United States supported his position throughout the Cold War, wilfully ignoring his opulent extravagance and helping protect his borders in exchange for help in combating communist movements in Angola and elsewhere, Mobutu's rule was not sustainable. He later made supercilious concessions to multiparty politics, but his behaviour was increasingly unpredictable and embarrassing to his western allies. He had outlived his strategic importance. Civil unrest grew, and in 1991 soldiers began looting in Kinshasa in protest at not being paid. By 1994 rates of inflation reached 1000 per cent: crippling in a country by now dependent on food imports. The public sector and much of the private sector were declared bankrupt. Looting sprees and riots became commonplace.

Tension in the Congo further increased following the 1994 Rwandan genocide. Paul Kagame's Tutsi-led Rwandan Patriotic Front had swept into power in Rwanda and one and a half million Hutu people sought refuge in camps in eastern Zaire. It was reported that Hutu militia forces (called *Interahamwe*) were using these camps to regroup, and Kagame was not prepared to tolerate this.

With support from Tanzania, Ethiopia, Eritrea and Angola, Kagame and Yoweri Museveni, by then the presidents of Rwanda and Uganda, created the Alliance of Democratic Forces for the Liberation of Congo (AFDL). In order to lend some Congolese authenticity to the 'liberation' effort Kagame and Museveni chose Laurent Kabila, a Congolese guerrilla fighter, as the spokesman of the AFDL—this despite his commonly recognised lack of leadership skills and history of violent banditry during his exile in Tanzania. The group also included many Congolese Tutsi who had faced prejudice in Zaire, including controversy over land rights since their emigration in the eighteenth century. Children were kidnapped in large numbers in the east of the country and taken to military training camps in Rwanda.

In 1996 the AFDL attacked from the east of the country, beginning the 'war of liberation'. Without his American and European allies, Mobutu could mount little defence. Wracked with guilt over the recent genocide (and scarred by the recent US intervention in Somalia), western leaders did little to challenge Kagame, and turned a blind eye to the atrocities committed by his proxy forces as they marched across the Congo. After a seven-month campaign and failed peace talks between Mobutu and Kabila in May 1997, Mobutu left Zaire. Kabila swept unopposed into Kinshasa and named himself president of the Democratic Republic of the Congo. Mobutu died of prostate cancer in Morocco later that year.

Once installed, Kabila was not willing to be Rwanda's puppet, nor was he keen to take the blame for the massacre of tens of thousands of Hutu refugees by Rwandan forces during the war of liberation. In August 1998 he expelled the Rwandans who had stayed in Kinshasa after the war. A week later, Rwanda attacked eastern Congo to start the Second Congo War, the deadliest conflict since the Second World War: over five million Congolese were to die, mainly from preventable diseases. Kabila, with the support of Zimbabwe, Chad, Namibia and Angola, fought the Congolese Rally for Democracy (Rassemblement Congolais pour la Démocratie, RCD), a proxy force created by Rwanda, Uganda and Burundi.

The frontline between these two main groups waxed and waned, but eventually came to pass through a small town called Lomela, in the very centre of the Congo. There, the two sides were separated by a river and by a bridge that was burnt to stumps in the fighting. Like the conflict elsewhere in the country, much of it was fought with locally-recruited proxy militias, which destroyed trust and multiplied conspiracy theories. Ten years after the war's end, and initially clueless of the history, we found ourselves in Lomela, subject to local conspiracies and 'arrested' at the behest of byzantine tribal politics, all whilst attempting to build a raft to float 9Bob and our kit across the former frontlines.

Returning to the war, a multitude of smaller guerrilla groups, including the Ugandan-backed Movement for the Liberation of Congo (MLC), led by the Congolese warlord Jean-Pierre Bemba, entered the fray as alliances fractured, collapsed and reformed. The accounts of the ever-more creative means of torture and brutal killings deployed during the conflict, including rape as a means of pulverising victims' insides, or forced auto-cannibalism, are bewildering and horrifying.

Fighting in the Congo was financed by captured diamond and coltan mines worked by forced labour. Kabila paid his foreign allies with the profits of the state-owned mining company Gécamines, while tolerating their systematic plundering of the stocks of minerals, timber, coffee and cattle they found in their occupied territories. He granted his allies mining concessions and exonerated them from taxes for all their business activities; he and his entourage kept healthy foreign bank accounts of their own. Meanwhile, in the year 2000 alone Rwanda exported $240 million worth of coltan extracted by Hutu prisoners of war.

In 2001 Laurent Kabila was murdered by his bodyguards. He was replaced by his son Joseph Kabila, who was quick to sue for peace. Many have since argued that the conflict was then deliberately prolonged by neighbouring countries in order to continue the looting of diamonds, copper, zinc and coltan. The war was finally brought to an end in 2003, after five years of fighting. It is estimated that three-quarters of the Congolese people were affected by the war either personally or due to the wider consequences of armed conflict (ICRC and Ipsos 2009). Despite widespread acknowledgement of the multitude of war crimes and human rights abuses that took place in the region during the two wars, there has been little progress by the international community in bringing the key actors to justice.

Joseph Kabila, former leader of the army of *kadogos* (child soldiers) during the First Congo War, was just thirty years old when he assumed the presidency. He had been trained at the National Defence University in Beijing, and was chief of the land forces during the Second Congo War. He was formally elected president of the DRC in 2006 and remains in power today following his (contested) re-election in 2011. Although elections are planned for 2016, Kabila has aired plans to remain president until a formal census can take place, and protests in Kinshasa against this scheme in early 2015 were firmly quashed.

The United Nations Organization Stabilization Mission in the Democratic Republic of the Congo (MONUSCO, previously MONUC) was first deployed to the DRC in 1999 to observe a ceasefire between the DRC and five regional states, as well as the disengagement of forces. Since then it has undergone several reorientations and re-formulations of its mandate. It remains active throughout the DRC with the mandate to support the government in its consolidation of peace, and to protect civilians, humanitarian personnel and human rights protectors from the imminent threat of physical violence. In March 2013 MONUSCO gained authorisation from the Security Council for a specialised 'intervention brigade' to strengthen peacekeeping efforts, particularly in the east of the country. Yet MONUSCO has been described somewhat alarmingly as 'ludicrously understaffed ... at times more interested in the perpetuation of the mission itself than the protection of the near-defenceless Congolese people' (Deibert 2013), and its mandate remains controversial. Our brief experiences with its personnel were of great kindness to us, but complete ineffectiveness in their mission.

More cynically, the DRC has been described as 'one of Africa's major development "markets"' (Trefon 2011). Major and minor international development agencies, aid workers and other non-governmental organisations compete to contribute, too often under 'greater pressure to commit money grandly than to spend it wisely' (Calderisi 2007). Either because of these efforts, or despite them, research since the early 1980s concludes that very little social, institutional or political reform has taken place. The DRC remains incredibly underdeveloped, with one of the highest rates of corruption in the world according to the World Bank, and some of the lowest indices of government effectiveness.

This corruption interferes in the rule of law and in the transparency of civil institutions, making private investment in such a country unattractive (Moyo 2010). Self-enrichment of the political elite remains the status quo, and army generals and parliamentarians alike requisition land and negotiate private agreements with foreign mining interests. According to academic literature about the country, international partners and Congolese authorities share responsibility for this state of affairs. Whilst civil servants and politicians 'deliberately hamper reform to stay in power', many key stakeholders have 'more vested interests in resisting reform than fostering it' (Trefon 2011). This sadly matches our experiences travelling through the country.

The UN admits that although national, regional and international efforts usually succeed in mitigating some of the worst effects of violence on the local population, they repeatedly fail to address the root causes of the recurrent violence (RNDH 2014). There is a focus on treating the more visible symptoms, rather than curing the disease. Stability in the region is still compromised by rebel groups including the March 23 Movement (M23), the Mai-Mai and the Ugandan Lord's Resistance Army. The report's authors argue that the key to lasting improvements in humanitarian conditions, economic growth and democracy is to rebuild a sense of national cohesion. The responsibility for this lies with the government of the DRC, which must accept responsibility for inclusive development, sustainable exploitation of natural resources, justice and equality, respect for human rights and equitable economic growth.

Meanwhile, China continues to strengthen relations with the DRC, working on the principle of mutual benefit. Relations date back to when Mobutu visited China in 1973 in order to diversify aid sources. In return, the Chinese built an 80,000-seat stadium in Kinshasa and the striking Palais du Peuple (parliament building), as well as a monumental pagoda in Mobutu's agricultural complex. Today China is the number one recipient of Congolese exports, and in return invests in mobile phone networks and infrastructure as well as funding scholarships for students to study in China. Military cooperation and arms deals also take place in the background. In response, the European Investment Bank warns that western banks are being undercut by Chinese banks which attach fewer social and environmental conditions to their loans—focusing on economic pragmatism rather than labour standards, environmental protection or contractual transparency.

In September 2007 the 'deal of the century' between Kinshasa and China took place. Characterised as an infrastructure for resources package, it originally amounted to nearly $10 billion. China agreed to build two hydroelectric dams, schools, roads and universities, and to fund a facelift for Kinshasa. In return, China received rights to 8 million tons of copper, 200,000 tons of cobalt and 372 tons of gold, as well as exemption from taxes and duties for thirty years. It was not discussed by parliament and little is known about the actual details and valuation assessments considered. Severe pressure from the IMF and World Bank, which feared that the DRC would be unable to repay its side and objected to the lack of conditions, forced a revision of the deal in 2009. The infrastructure commitments from China were reduced to $3 billion (from $6 billion), depriving the DRC of much needed funds, though protecting the government from potentially unserviceable debt in the future.

In his well-researched examination of why aid is not fixing the Congo, Theodore Trefon uses the Parable of the Scorpion and the Crocodile to frame his discussion (Trefon 2011). This is an animal fable that has been used in different contexts to summarise the situation in the Middle East, and many troubled areas along the River Nile over many centuries. It has been associated with ancient Persian art, Jewish lore and Indian tradition, and has been used by many children's writers, most notably Roald Dahl. Having crossed the Congo, we have borrowed its use from Trefon to frame our story. We will return to it in the conclusion.

The Crocodile and the Scorpion: A Congolese Parable

One afternoon in Kinshasa, a scorpion asked his friend the crocodile to help him cross the majestic River Congo. 'I have to cross over to Brazzaville but don't know how to swim. As you swim with such ease and elegance, let me climb on your back so we can leave without further ado.' The crocodile replied: 'Dear scorpion, I know you and the reputation of your kind. Once we get to the middle of the river, you'll sting me and we'll both drown.' 'Why would I ever do such a thing?' asked the scorpion. 'If I sting you and you die, I'll drown with you.' The crocodile thought for a moment and agreed to help the scorpion. 'Climb on: let's get moving before nightfall.'

They left the shore and headed for Brazzaville. As the lights of Kinshasa started to fade and their destination appeared on the horizon, the scorpion had a sudden urge and stung the valiant swimmer in the neck. 'Why did you do that?' asked the crocodile, who was nearing the end of his tether. 'I'm exhausted; we're never going to make it!'

Just before they both disappeared under the murky water, the scorpion whispered: 'That's the way it is. This is Congo. Don't try to understand.'

This brief outline sets the context for the story that follows. It is the story of three journeys: a physical journey across some of the toughest terrain in the world, a complex navigation through the multiple logics and complicated psychology of the Congolese peoples, and an interpersonal journey of three friends in a very old car. The journey challenged all of our preconceptions about the DRC and our own understandings of ourselves. It is full of examples of ridiculous physical challenges, exceptional kindness and inhuman unhelpfulness from those whom we met along the way.

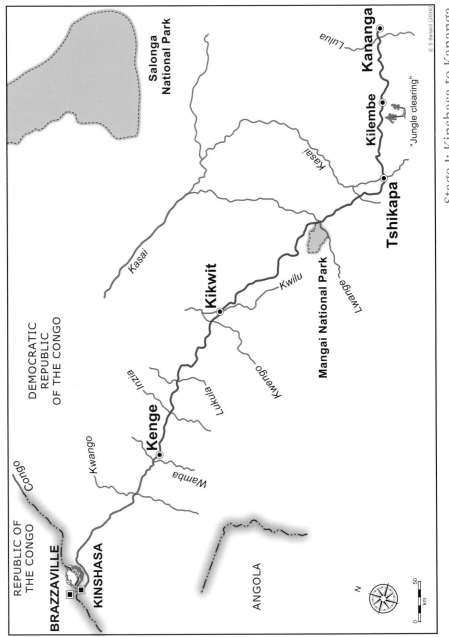

Stage 1: Kinshasa to Kananga

REPUBLIC OF
THE CONGO

DEMOCRATIC
REPUBLIC
OF THE CONGO

BRAZZAVILLE

KINSHASA

Congo

Kwango

Kenge

Wamba

Lukula

Kwango

Kwilu

Kikwit

Mangai National Park

Lwange

Kasai

Kasai

Salonga
National Park

Tshikapa

Kilembe

Kananga

Lulua

"Jungle clearing"

ANGOLA

N

0   50
km

© S Ballard (2016)

Chapter 1

Kinshasa

Day 1: (first night in DRC) Brazzaville to Louozi - 138 miles
Day 2: Louozi to Kinshasa - 211 miles
Days 3-11: Remained in Kinshasa - 123 miles

So that is how the three of us—Chloe, Charlie and I—found ourselves in Kinshasa with a very old, very broken Land Rover. I'm a former army officer and acted as the mechanic and Chloe's a doctor. We'd already spent four months driving from London to Kinshasa through West Africa. Charlie, a photojournalist, had just flown in. Originally the plan had been to put 9Bob on a barge and float him upstream to Kisangani, from where we would drive to South Sudan. It would take a month we thought—three weeks on the boat and a week on the road. We had been covering an average of 100 miles a day on the road up to this point. It would be reasonably easy; the only issues would be drinking water on the boat and the Lord's Resistance Army, who were said to be kidnapping people in the area that we were going to drive through. Not ideal, but we would deal with it when we got to it. This turned out to be the motif for the whole trip.

Instead, the next two months would see us drive from Kinshasa to Juba covering an average of forty miles a day. The total mileage covered crossing the DRC was 2,494 miles, from Louozi in the south-west to the South Sudanese border town of Laso in the north-east.

Kinshasa completely changed our plans. Firstly, 9Bob was in a bad way. The twenty-seven-year-old Land Rover 90 had just travelled some 15,000 miles over some of the worst roads imaginable. While travelling back from the airport where we had picked up Charlie the brakes completely failed, causing a car crash (our only collision in Africa) and necessitating some creative driving across a junction or two. We wound up in a Jesuit mission, where the kind French Supreme Father allowed 9Bob to stay. The next morning we had a long list of things that we needed to fix—Charlie had brought out a spare fuel tank, for instance, as the old one had been leaking since Sierra Leone. The bearings in all the wheels were shot. The universal joints were rattling again. The steering guard was bent beyond recognition. We had recently replaced the bush on the suspension but feared it might be failing, and we'd lost yet another bump stop on the crossing from ROC.

We set about doing what we could to get him roadworthy. Not MOT standard, but solid and safe(ish) and ready to cross the Congo. Kinshasa was a busy time: long days working on 9Bob followed by one or two long nights in a rum bar favoured by expats. The expats were incredulous when we told them we had just driven from London. Their perception of life outside the compound as dangerous, dirty and threatening jarred with our experiences of humour and hospitality along the way. But Kinshasa, the largest French-speaking city in the world, is an amazing place bursting with life and music. They missed out on cheerful backstreet bars, delicious street BBQs and the colourful hubbub of the local markets. Instead, most expats moved from one

expensive, air-conditioned and guarded restaurant to the next in white SUVs. They utterly distorted the economy of the city that they lived in, but barely touched. No-one, anywhere, would accept less than a $5 note. To spend less you had to use Congolese francs, which expats didn't use.

Luckily for us, Kinshasa was full of spare parts and was home to a helpful Nigerian named Power (not a nickname). Power welded most of 9Bob back together outside his revivalist church, which he tried to get us to join. We glossed over the fact that Charlie was a Muslim and made plans to have a look at a service. Kinshasa would have been a lot more difficult without Power's kindness, his time, his warmth and his firm belief in miracles. Unlike the lamp-lit, tarmacked, three-lane roads of shiny UN vehicles, disciplined traffic policemen and London-priced restaurants, Power and other displaced people came from a more African part of town. Here we found sewage-filled potholes that could sink a 4WD, shoe-less children, university graduates making omelettes beside the road and cripples with flip flops on their hands. Believing in miracles was a necessity for daily life.

We were in Kinshasa for about ten days, crisscrossing the town and trying to avoid paying bribes—in one short journey of about five miles we were stopped four times. After the third time even Power started arguing with the policeman, telling them that it was not right to ask us for money just because we were here, and white skinned (we had made very sure our paperwork was completely in order). At first he had thought I was exaggerating when I told him of our usual treatment by the police.

Our guidebook claimed that it was impossible to travel in the Congo without paying bribes. 'They [the Congolese] are the most corrupt people on earth.' It even advised that it was impossible to get anything done without paying a bribe. How was the country meant to advance if this is what progressive, enlightened foreigners were writing about it? Up until this point, and all through West Africa, Chloe and I hadn't paid any bribes, and we weren't about to start. It became quickly evident, though, that in Kinshasa we were alone in holding onto this principle. Ironically, there was so much money in the capital that we couldn't have afforded the bribe prices demanded, and maybe that's why, after we repeatedly and politely declined the offer to hand over cash or pretended not to understand, they always let us go.

In-between trips around town with Power trying to find obscure gaskets, welding brake pipes and bruising our knuckles on 9Bob, we investigated the barge to Kisangani.

'Sure, I'll give you a call tomorrow,' said Emmanuel, the boat captain, drawing deeply on a mug of *jus de maïs*, a very raw local spirit. It was nine -thirty in the morning. We would never really get over the extent of casual alcoholism in the Congo, but as we went further into our journey it made more and more sense. Life for most was backbreaking and devoid of any hope. In those circumstances, many of us would turn to alcohol.

Emmanuel never did call back, and we found later that the next boat going to Kisangani would be in three weeks. There then occurred a scene, oft-repeated over the next two months. We would pull out the maps, trace our route and convince ourselves that it could be done. We would then try to ask as many people as possible about the route, and no-one would know anything. Or worse, they would authoritatively tell us completely opposing stories. We would shrug and realise that we had no choice. We even went to the British embassy to find out more information. We were there anyway because Charlie had lost his passport.

This had necessitated a trip to the police station in Gombe, an upmarket district of Kinshasa, where all the international NGOs and embassies were based. We needed to report the passport lost. We were ushered into the chief's office, musty with mould and lit only by light from the glassless window, where we explained our problem. He then demanded to see Charlie's passport, as was his right as a policeman. 'But it's lost,' Charlie said.

'If you can't show your passport, you must pay a fine.'

Chloe burst out laughing and went to buy some Cokes, leaving Charlie and I to deal with this slightly rotund man. Finally the problem was solved with the gentle threat of involving the British embassy. A deputy set to work writing the report on an ancient typewriter that he had to borrow from the town council secretaries down the road. It was not lost on us that Gombe was the centre of the international intervention in the DRC, and after a decade of effort the police did not even have proper electricity, any computers or appropriate offices. Once we had the letter, we headed back to the embassy.

'So, you're telling me there is no way that you can get me another passport inside of eight weeks?' said Charlie, shivering in the air-conditioned embassy vestibule.

The Congolese woman working at the embassy shrugged, as if to say, 'it's your own fault for losing it you fool'. It seemed like the trip would not get off the ground: without Charlie we wouldn't be able to get across the country. It was too big, too undeveloped, too raw. The Democratic Republic of Congo really is one of the most bureaucratic, officious and corrupt countries in the world. There were hundreds of checkpoints between us and South Sudan. An Emergency Travel Document, which they offered us, simply would not cut it, and it definitely would not get us into South Sudan.

Despondent, we returned to the car outside and I began to fix something recently broken underneath. By a stroke of good luck, and we were to have equal amounts of catastrophic luck over the coming weeks, a British woman called Claire (not her real name) walked past and, attracted by 9Bob's number plate, stopped to chat. As I tinkered, Chloe and Charlie explained what we were trying to do: it turned out her husband worked in the embassy and she was sure that he would be able to give us some advice. At that point, Charlie's phone rang. It was a street cigarette seller, one step above beggar in the poverty rankings: he had found Charlie's passport and rang the number inside. 'Did he want it back?'

We raced across town to get the passport and gave the cigarette seller two months' salary. Honesty, we agreed, should be rewarded. So should stupidity: Chloe, the mother of the group, confiscated the passport from Charlie for the remainder of the trip. We then raced back to our meeting at the embassy, for which we were late, because something else broke on 9Bob. The British official looked at us sceptically and asked whether we should be attempting a trip across the Congo when we couldn't even get across Kinshasa. We sheepishly explained that they were 'teething problems'.

The official, a good man stepping outside of his remit to help us, didn't really have much information: 'Don't go there, it's dangerous, and anyway, we don't have a footprint outside of Kinshasa or the east [where there was a war between the government, the UN and various rebel groups]. It would be impossible for us to help you if there were any problems.' I think we had been expecting more, that the British government that was spending millions annually in the country on reconstruction and development would know more.

He did, however, put us in touch with a British army officer who was serving with the UN in the north-east of the country. This was incredibly useful as having just left the army I could hopefully rely on a brother officer to help us out. We arranged a completely unofficial checking-in schedule with him. As we left, he reiterated the official advice—don't go!—and then grinned, shook our hands and wished us luck. That evening, as we were walking back from a bar to the church mission where we were staying, some stoned Congolese soldiers tried unsuccessfully to rob us.

We filled 9Bob with everything imaginable. Food for a month; 150 litres of fuel; as many spare parts as we could find; a new gas canister for our stove. We also stocked up the medical kit with intravenous fluids, a variety of malaria treatments, iodine and other sundries as we supposed that it might take several days to get to any kind of medical facility. In the meantime all we would have would be Chloe's skills and what we had with us. It was already evident that she would have her work cut out—Charlie had arrived in the Congo stating that he wouldn't be taking malaria prophylaxis because 'it just wasn't for him'. Then again, he had also turned up with only white t-shirts, a pale blue jumper and Brylcreem for his hair. He clearly saw our forthcoming trip as some sort of Grand Tour.

It had taken Chloe nearly a week to persuade Charlie that he had a responsibility to the rest of the group to take the malaria drugs she'd trawled around town to find for him. It was alarmingly difficult to know for certain that medicines bought in Kinshasa were authentic, and it had taken her some

effort to track down a reputable pharmacist. We had had similar discussions about eating bush meat. Charlie was up for it (he was up for most things) until we explained about Ebola and the variety of other diseases that you could catch. He actually looked disappointed that he would have to take his malaria pills and not eat monkeys; to him it seemed much less adventurous, and adventure was why he was in the Congo.

Chloe had read that you needed movement permits and even photo permits in the DRC, so we went to the appropriate ministries. Thankfully the movement permits had just been abolished, but not so the photo permits. It took a whole day. We had to visit six offices several times, drop by the bank, and get our paperwork signed by the minister of tourism himself. All of this accompanied by a small man in a dusty suit from the northern Kivus. An economic migrant to Kinshasa who was unable to afford the boat passage back home, he vociferously advocated our status as guests each time a colleague tried to short change us. In the event, no-one outside Kinshasa asked us for the photo permit until our last day in the Congo, and everyone asked us for our movement permit. There was a total disconnect between Kinshasa and the rest of the country, but we never really bottomed out how much of it was an actual disconnect and how much of it was invented to suit our interlocutors' purposes. We were still learning.

That day we also found ourselves in the hilarious situation where the Congolese officials ranked us for our French-speaking skills. The three of us were crammed into a tiny cubby hole of an office with two officials and a secretary, sitting carefully to avoid disturbing dusty stacks of musty paperwork. They were officials in a random part of the Congolese bureaucracy that needed to sign our photo permit application form. Originally we had all begun by speaking in turn during different parts of the negotiation, but then it became obvious that everyone was getting confused. We asked them if they understood us. Thoughtfully, they passed comment on our French: Chloe's was judged to be 'très clair, excellent' (very clear, excellent), I was below this with 'rugueux mais compréhensible' (rough but understandable) and Charlie got 'confus et trop compliqué' (confused and too complicated)!

We spent our last night in a hotel: we had been bedding down with the DRC national cycling team in the church mission. They seemed a fairly professional bunch and would have lectures and practice races—this was their annual training camp. However, the facilities were not up to catering for that number of people and the toilets had become an alarming experience. We moved to a cheap hotel for the last night, but it still cost $90 a room. Kinshasa had been really expensive because we had had to spend so much on the car and on the victualling. We only had a couple of thousand dollars of cash reserves, but spending $180 on our last 'luxury' was worth every cent.

Alone together for the first time in a week, Chloe challenged me on the state of our ailing relationship. It was becoming clear to both of us that we were falling out of love. Three days before, we had had our four-year anniversary. Originally we had planned to celebrate it, but it had passed, unremarked. We were seriously on the rocks. As we lay on the bed in a ridiculous velvet-wallpapered hotel room, we looked into the abyss. Chloe was understandably afraid to plunge into the Congo with the emotional uncertainties hanging over us, but I was unable to reassure her that it would be ok.

Coupled with this were other feelings and other drives. We had both come so far on this trip, and we were reluctant to give up on the opportunity of driving across the Congo. We both knew that we would never be in this situation again in our lives, and that there was no way of getting across the Congo without all three of us. We were going to complete what we started. We agreed to continue talking about it, but it was horribly painful. Chloe later commented that that was the only time that she had seen me cry, apart from at my beloved grandmother's funeral. The next morning we set out.

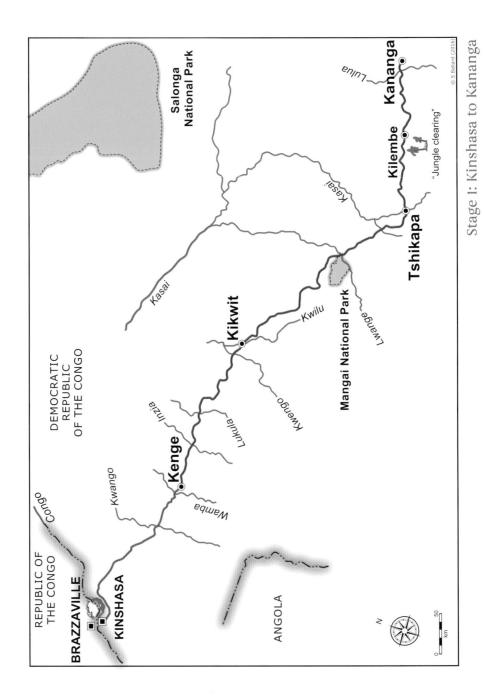

Stage 1: Kinshasa to Kananga

Chapter 2

Kinshasa to Kananga

Day 12: Kinshasa to east of Mutiene - 95 miles
Day 13: East of Mutiene to east of Kikwit - 232 miles
Day 14: East of Kikwit to east of Mukendi - 107 miles
Day 15: East of Mukendi to east of Samba - 20 miles
Day 16: East of Samba to GRID - 30 miles
Day 17: GRID to east of Katanga - 50 miles
Day 18: East of Katanga to east of Tshikapa - 37 miles
Day 19: East of Tshikapa to GRID (jungle clearing) - 14 miles
Day 20-26: GRID (Day 22 Mike leaves, Day 25 Mike back)
Day 27: GRID to Kananga - 125 miles

The route we had chosen was not particularly complicated in that there was not much of a choice. The Congolese travel by boat. The few who can afford to travel by plane. No-one travels by road if they can possibly avoid it, or unless the journey is thoroughly local.

Most people thought we were lying when we told them that we were travelling across the country to Juba. There are only two north-south routes on the maps and one of them runs through a war zone in the east. The UN (MONUSCO) had just put an extra brigade of troops through that part of the country, complete with attack helicopters. We had decided to take the other route, directly though the centre or the 'heart' of the country. There were three legs of roughly equal lengths, each about 750 miles (this was also our fuel endurance with the extra jerry cans on a decent road). Firstly, from Kinshasa to Kananga. We would have to take the slightly longer route via Tshikapa because we'd heard the bridge was down at Ilebo and everyone was on diversion. We'd also been told that much of this was actually on a road, and so we factored in about a week. Second, Kananga to Kisangani, across the centre. No-one knew anything about this section of the route. Two weeks. Why not? Surely we would be able to cover fifty or so miles in a day? The last section, back on our old route, would take a week from Kisangani to South Sudan. We'd heard that the UN was working on the road up there.

We set off along Route Nationale No.1. We had to pay official tolls, but didn't mind—the road was good quality. It rolled gracefully through green plains with intermittent villages alongside the roads or set back down dusty red-yellow tracks.

It was great to be moving again after all the setbacks in Kinshasa. We spent the first night with a dope-smoking soldier living in a tent in a massive Congolese army training area, with only a scarecrow for company. What he was guarding we never managed to find out, but he did spend a few weeks there at a time guarding it. He joked that it was better than the east as he begged things from us. Jean-Pierre was a decent man who had nothing, but this encounter was a polite form of what became immensely tiring for us in the Congo: slightly aggressive and/or insistent begging from everyone.

They all had a point—the poverty was astounding, and we'd have liked to be able to give them the clothes from our backs—which people often requested. But had we done so, we would have had nothing ourselves: we were only three, and a car, and they were legion, and every item that we had we needed for the unknown unknowns that we might face on the journey. It is easy to say now that you should treat the last beggar like the first, and we tried very hard to be polite or make a joke of it, but the truth is that we progressively failed to live up to our own ideals and sometimes we were very rude.

The next day we moved on early. Almost immediately we ran into our first police checkpoint. There were to be seven that day.

They didn't ask for a bribe. We just had to register ourselves. In three different books. It took half an hour. We drove away, and hit another checkpoint at the other side of the town. The process was repeated. They asked for a bribe, and we declined. We were allowed to continue. These police were well used to foreigners because there were a number of development projects along the road sponsored by organisations like the World Bank, World Vision and the UK's Department for International Development (DFID). In some of the villages, boards from several different NGOs seemed to be competing for space along the roadside. They were doing everything from education to hand-washing, sanitation to community empowerment. Gradually, as we got further from Kinshasa, the boards started to disappear, and the Congolese were left to fend for themselves.

The second night we stayed in a quarry from which material was excavated to make the road. We didn't realise until after we had set up camp that it was also used as a toilet by most of the local population. By that point it was dark and so we cleaned the ground for our mosquito dome and tent and got on with our night routine. As usual we were untroubled by people during the night, though we were frequently disturbed by a young pig, seemingly attracted to our camp by the sound of my snoring.

The next morning we discovered oil leaking out of the gearbox because the plug seal had broken. In our treasure trove of spare parts was some cork sheet, and in an episode reminiscent of a children's TV programme Charlie spent several hours cutting and shaping the cork to the exact size to re-seal the bolt on the underside of the box. My reasoning, which Chloe quickly supported, was that he had done design technology at school and so was best suited to the task. He then lost the round of paper-scissors-stone and had to lie on the ground in the poo working on the oily underside of 9Bob. Unfortunately, we had lost a lot of transmission fluid.

We had only been driving a few hours that morning when the road just stopped. It stopped just after a village with absolutely no warning. Road works, the villagers said. Beyond the end of the road was a track with twenty-inch deep ruts caused by giant orange mining trucks. I edged 9Bob to the end of the road and it was immediately clear that the ruts were too deep, and too far apart, for us to use the track. Chloe began talking to some villagers who explained a diversion to us: if we followed this track, and then that track, we would get to Tshikapa in a day. From there, the road began again and we would get to Kananga in a couple of days. In the event, it would be nearly twelve days before we got to Kananga.

I span the car round and set off down the side track, slightly annoyed at the setback. The track was sandy, but once we lowered the pressures in our tyres (which gives them a greater contact surface area with the ground) we were soon moving along well. Heading out across savannah-like terrain, we frequently crossed small fords or streams. Often leaving these were women carrying buckets of water back to their villages: despite the proximity to Kinshasa, there were few bore holes or pumps in the area. We were completely off our maps, navigating by compass, and so at each village we came to one of us asked the direction to Tshikapa. We kept getting lost and having to retrace our steps. In one village we stopped and Charlie asked for directions from a policeman who was just standing by the side of the road waiting for something. Slightly bizarrely, there was a prisoner handcuffed to him who politely gave us excellent directions in clear French. We drove off leaving them standing there peacefully.

We returned to the main road, approaching it from ninety degrees. A man who had dismounted from his motorbike to cross the knee-high ruts explained to us that the mess we were looking at actually was the Route Nationale. It resembled what one imagines the surface of the moon to be like. Because of the state of the road there were small diversions through villages, but in the end we kept returning to the massive sandy ruts. In each village we asked for directions, and every time we did people said they would not help us till we paid them. None of us had ever encountered this, anywhere. It exposed an aspect of the Congolese character that was clearly the result of their appalling treatment by outsiders over the last two centuries. When we refused to pay, they would laugh, adding: 'Then you will suffer'.

Later on this became an oft-repeated phrase: many Congolese are constantly telling you how much they are suffering, and in most cases they really are suffering. 'Nous souffrons' is an exceptionally common phrase, akin to a national narrative. 'Regardez la souffrance!' is another variation on the theme. We all dealt with this aspect of the journey in different ways. Chloe in particular felt confused by the simultaneous compassion and irritation it gave rise to. It never really seemed to bother Charlie, but nothing much does. For that reason he features less in the text than Chloe and I: despite being a constant, invaluable presence he did not (or does not) engage with his emotions verbally. His narrative is instead writ large in the beautiful photos spread through these pages.

We discussed various options for tackling the route. 'Ok,' I said, 'how about we try and see if we can move along the ruts with one wheel in the rut and the other balanced on the middle bit between the ruts?' It was a suggestion with serious consequences.

We made some progress slowly, trying our suspension to the limit as we leaned precariously to one side, then the other, and then beached the car in the middle of the next village. Surrounded by shouting and laughing villagers we dug the hard compacted sand from under the car and continued. This happened six more times before the sun began to set. Once we got trapped in a gully and met a lorry coming the other way. Without discussion they began to hook 9Bob up to their lorry with a steel towing cable in order to pull us out.

Fearful that it would rip out the underside of 9Bob, to which they shrugged, I had to physically face them down while the others dug to free us. That evening we stopped at the side of the road to camp and put up our mosquito dome and tent in a state of grubby exhaustion. We had the first (of many) councils of war: we had poor maps and an unhelpful, mocking population, and the clearance on our vehicle (which until this point had been more than sufficient) would not cut it on a road that had been mauled by big mining lorries.

To make it worse, 9Bob was beginning to stink: many Congolese villages had been using the impassable Route Nationale as a toilet, and the human excrement was being flicked up against the car. That didn't seem to deter the children, though, who were using our car as a moving climbing frame. In every village that we drove through we would be mobbed by hundreds of children and adolescents. As far as we could tell, they far outnumbered the adults, even accepting that adults would be more likely to be working away from the village during the day. As we drove into a village, they would climb on the car, jump in front of it or try and hang onto the roof rack. Several times we would have to continue through the village with one of us standing on the roof as if to fend off boarders.

There was no malice in their actions—jumping on our car was fun, and they were going to do it, no matter how much we begged/cajoled/threatened them not to. From our point of view, the things they tended to hang onto—like the roof ladder and the tyre on the back door—were somewhat fragile and we could not really afford to be without them. The back door, bent by their weight, was already beginning to come away from the frame and Chloe struggled to open it. We were also very aware that if there was an accident we would be to blame in the eyes of the community, regardless of the circumstances. It was our continual nightmare that a toddler might get trapped under our wheels and be killed, especially since they were difficult to spot as they squatted to go to the toilet among the deep ridges of the so-called road.

Chloe was also feeling particularly lethargic and emotional. We thought that it might be related to the strain of our relationship difficulties, but a week later, when she was back to normal, she retrospectively self-diagnosed with concussion following a blow to the head—at one point the waffle boards had slammed into the back of her head as we beached ourselves in a rut. (Waffle boards are hard lattice boards of reinforced plastic which can take the weight of the vehicle.) She'd also been suffering with nausea and dizziness, but, confused about the cause, had been reluctant to tell us. We took note—we needed to be more careful, and we needed to communicate our ailments to each other, irrespective of whatever else was going on between us. This was a timely reminder of the value, and precariousness, of our health. Our strength to dig and push and pull was crucial, as was the skill and knowledge of our team medic. Around this time we all made the effort to cross-train each other on our particular skill sets. Charlie taught us how to prepare sugar cane.

The next day we decided on a change of tack. We would go back to trying to find smaller cross-country paths that we could navigate on in an attempt to get to Tshikapa. We even spent some of this day navigating directly across the landscape using compass and GPS, and occasionally having to create the route in front of us with shovel or waffle boards. We were still in an area of grassland that had originally been primary rainforest. At some point in the last few years it had been cleared by fire, but it remained tortuous terrain with unseen dips and gullies. It took us almost half the day to find the first suitable path off the main road, by which point we had dug ourselves out of the ground several more times.

When we got on a path in the afternoon we sped along and made some decent progress. But we were tired from the morning's digging, and in one critical village we didn't ask for directions. The track began to get narrower and narrower. We knew that we were heading towards a river, the same river that ran through Tshikapa, and we were told by a passer-by that we would be able to cross the river at the point at which we would meet it—so we continued. We confirmed with another person the name of the village we were heading towards, unaware that besides the village marked on our map there were two others in the area with the same name.

The track was completely hemmed in on both sides by low trees and scrubby forest and it was getting increasingly narrow. Parts of the path were washed away, so we would first ride high on one side and then high on the other. In a couple of places we had to get out the waffle boards and create tracks to take us over big drops or gullies in the route. At many points the vehicle was balanced right on its lateral tipping point—a move to the right or left would have had us on our side. The concentration required to keep us upright was exhausting for the driver and terrifying for the passengers, who occasionally had to hang on the outside of the vehicle to keep it balanced.

The further we went the more uneasy we became. It was getting dark, the path was disappearing, and more than three people in a row had told us that either the path would become too narrow or we would not be able to cross the river when we got to it. A simple vote, demonstrating the beauty of having three of us on the trip, decided that we should turn back and try to make it to the main road. We had done twenty miles that day, about half of it down this track in the wrong direction. It was utterly dispiriting. The track was so narrow that we couldn't turn the car round and had to reverse it for about a mile. Eventually we found somewhere we could edge slightly into the forest and string up our hammocks for the night. We were thoroughly disheartened. Worse, we were running out of gin. This was proving to be much more difficult than we expected. In West Africa, there had at least been tracks to travel on, but here we were moving on pedestrian paths or cross country, and over appalling terrain. We had a fire that night and sat around talking in low voices.

We thought there was a chance we could get to Tshikapa that day and so the next morning we tried to get off as early as possible. There was a limit to how early this could be: we were almost on the equator so it only got light at about six. Once up, there was a fair amount of camp admin to do. Someone would get the breakfast on—invariably tea and porridge with milk powder—while another would strike the camp and the third would run through a series of checks on the vehicle. Although I was the 'mechanic', everyone was trained on how to do the daily checks and a few other simple procedures.

Once off, we sped along the path back to the main road. Again we decided on a change of tack: we would stick to the main road and deal with the ruts and poo as best we could. It was that morning that some poo got flicked onto Charlie's cheek as he sat in the passenger seat, which meant that Chloe, who was driving, had to stop the car as she was laughing so hard. We found him a wet-wipe (strictly rationed by this point). It contrasted beautifully with his carefully arranged coiffure.

Eventually we found our way back to the main road, which had been pisted (compacted with a roller) as it grew closer to the boundary with Kasai-Occidental province. The boundary between the provinces was a relatively small river and, we found, crossable by a new Chinese bridge built in 2011. It was very strange seeing a shiny new piece of infrastructure when we hadn't seen anything new, or metal, since Kinshasa. The surrounding areas were full of diamond and gold mines.

The 'town' of Louange on the other side was the first settlement larger than a small village that we had seen since leaving the tarmacked road. The prices were about double what they were in Kinshasa (beer, for example, went from $1 to $2). It reinforced a very important lesson about the Congo: it is utterly devoid of an effective transport network. Looking around, it was clear that most of the goods in the market were unaffordable to most of the people who lived in the town. They were to sell to the lorries that plied the route between Kinshasa and Kananga. These transport everything, including up 20,000 litres of fuel in palm oil containers (the fuel also doubles in price between Kinshasa and Kananga). Unfortunately for us, the main road disappeared again in the town. It had been so cut up by trucks that it looked like there had also been some sort of landslip in the town: it was utterly impassable. I went forward on foot to try to scout out a path. Charlie went to register us with the local officials as we had to do everywhere. It took him over an hour.

While Chloe and I were waiting for Charlie, people were repeatedly coming up to us and asking for things, or pointing at things in the vehicle and saying 'donnez-moi ça'. We walked around looking for a water pump as we were short of water, but returned to the car thwarted, having found only a crowd of young boys crowded around a man roasting a piglet on coals. Finally we got away and then camped for the night about ten miles short of Tshikapa. The road still required us to balance one wheel in the rut and the other on the raised centre, and we were still beaching ourselves regularly, blunting our shovels against the compacted dirt.

It was very odd finally entering Tshikapa. It had only been six days since we left Kinshasa, but we felt like we had had to fight almost every inch of the way (the road out of Kinshasa had been forgotten in the exertions of the last three days). We were pretty exhausted by the combination of long days, hot sun, a lot of shovel work and some fairly obtuse officials and members of the public. I parked 9Bob and we got out a little shell-shocked and wandered around. Chloe decided that we needed a cold drink and Charlie found a shop. We all started putting things onto the counter that we thought we would need for the upcoming journey and before long we had a small pile of stuff, including a crate of soft drinks. The shopkeeper had clearly seen us coming and quoted a price that wasn't far off the London price. We were so dazed that we almost paid it before I snapped myself awake and stopped the sale. We left with three cans of warm fizzy drink: the 'bright lights' and civilisation of Tshikapa were having an effect after the last few days.

Focusing on what we really needed, we walked up to a group of men who were standing next to a pile of fuel drums and jerry cans. We wanted about a hundred litres. This was far more than we needed to get to Kananga, but we had decided that we should stock everything up to full at every opportunity that we got—we had seen how little there was out in the countryside. The guy started off quoting a ludicrous price: enough to build him a new house if we bought the full hundred litres from him.

While I negotiated with the growing crowd, a Congolese man came up to the other side of the car and spoke to Chloe in English with a Chinese accent. Very bizarre. He'd worked in a mine. Slightly surreally, people in the villages had also started shouting 'Nin Hao' at us as we passed, assuming that we were Chinese. We guessed that we must have been the only non-Chinese foreigners in this part of the country for a while: we were just entering the diamond and gold mining area. As the top recipient of Congolese exports worldwide, the Chinese have a strong network of public and private mineral-extraction facilities.

At last I managed to agree a decent price of about $1.50 per litre. Once that was settled, I casually asked him what the quality of the fuel was like and, of course, he stated that his fuel was 'pure'. 'Then you won't mind if we put it through our filter first, and anything that the filter rejects we won't pay for?' By now there was a crowd surrounding our little negotiation and he was trapped. If he was selling watered down fuel (a very common practice in the DRC), then he would also be selling it to the locals for their generators. Chloe had been given the tip before we left by a friend who worked for Médecins Sans Frontières: always use a fuel/water separation filter. We don't think our fuel seller had ever seen one judging by the look on his face when we returned 15 per cent of his product back to him because it was water. I still wonder how he explained it to all the other people in the crowd as we drove away.

The good news was that it was probably two days to Kananga and the government was doing some work on the road. Apparently the terrible ruts caused by the lorries had been filled in. This was a big relief: it would be a while before we could leave as we still needed to find somewhere to wash and to pick up some drinking water. Tshikapa was a town split by a very steep-banked river, and we crossed over to the other half trying to find somewhere where we could get access to the water. The best spot seemed to be in the middle of an old Belgian works yard full of early 1900s rail, river and mining equipment slowly rusting away. Locomotives stamped with 'Antwerp: 1934' lay on their sides. This was the first time that we had seen this, but the more we penetrated into the interior the more common it became, with rusted machinery emerging from dirt paths in towns or spotted between houses as a familiar part of the landscape. In many respects it was like being an archaeologist discovering some ancient civilisation.

The DRC had been at its most 'advanced' state just before the Belgians left. There was a functioning, paved road network (our route, for instance, had been fully paved). There was also a rail network, remnants of which still existed now. We repeatedly came across these machinery graveyards that told the story of a much richer Congo, even though those riches were built on the lives of the Congolese people. You could make out the landing docks on the river, with mechanical lift equipment to lift cargo onto a ski-lift type affair, which raised the cargo to the level of the works yards, where it could be warehoused or loaded onto trains. Of course, that process stripped the Congo of its raw materials and its population was subjected to appalling depredations by the colonial 'masters'. There were so many juxtapositions of thought it was hard to know what to think. The Congo was now free; but it was fucked. It was eerie.

A section of the warehouses in the ex-works yard had been turned into a school, and we were immediately surrounded by students and teachers. The teachers jostled the adolescents out of the way, making their way to the front of the crowd so they could be the first to ask us for money. Ignoring our muddy clothes and dirty bodies, they invited us to come and 'talk about how you can help us'. To be fair to them, the last foreigners who had arrived at their school had probably been development workers, with whom they confused us. We, however, begged to be allowed to wash.

The warehouse had a long cable car arrangement going down to the river, which, like everything, was slowly rusting into the mud. We scrambled down the river cliff and began to wash alongside hundreds of other people for whom this was their laundry, bath and source of drinking water. Even though we were filtering our drinking water through a micro pump, we were not willing to use the brown, sudsy waters as a source so we set out to find another as we headed east out of the town. Luckily this was relatively easy—someone had sunk a concrete tube into the ground over a source and, through taking photos and showing people the screen on the back of the camera, Charlie managed to negotiate us a few buckets full.

The road east out of Tshikapa was made of compressed aggregate and we drove along marvelling at its smoothness. It was less than 150 miles to Kananga and we would probably make it at some point the following day. In good spirits,

Chloe made us sardine and avocado sandwiches for a late lunch—bread and fresh vegetables were a rare treat. But it was not to last and the road slowly deteriorated until we were back to the same deep, car- and morale-breaking sand ruts. Frequently we were tempted to try and drive 'off road' across the scorched areas of cleared scrub: being small-scale farmers, the Congolese frequently moved on, leaving large wastelands behind. But they never dug up the roots and stumps of the vegetation, and we were unable to pass over the spiky obstacles. Thankfully, this time there was a parallel track about half a mile to the south of the 'highway' that we could use. It was just wide enough for 9Bob. We had to drive very carefully because it went through villages and tiny children, pigs and chickens would regularly run out into our path. But we made better progress and, most importantly, there was no digging.

Bang!

Chloe had been driving at about fifteen miles per hour, and had gone straight into a tree on the right hand side of the track. We got out, slightly dazed, and began to mock her until Charlie noticed that fluid was leaking out of the bottom of the engine block. He reached in the back of the vehicle and grabbed a plastic

box which he put under the leak to catch as much of the fluid as possible. We couldn't really afford to lose it at this stage. It was red, which meant that it was coming out of the power steering and was Automatic Transmission Fluid (ATF). I barely knew anything about the power steering, as it was one of the systems that I had not yet had to fix.

Having undone the bonnet (it was secured with a rope as the catch was broken) I could see that fluid was streaming out of a cracked pipe in-between two components in the power steering system. That looked like something I could fix, but first we had to get the car back onto the track. Chloe went to straighten the wheels so that Charlie and I could push 9Bob back onto the track. The steering wheel was frozen—there was movement in it down the steering column until it reached the steering box, at which point it locked. We jacked the car up and it was the same story—the road wheels would move slightly, but when you got to the steering box it was blocked. By this point young men were starting to assemble around us. In the claustrophobic tropical forest alley one of us was on permanent duty as crowd controller, occasionally exchanging pleasantries or information, but mainly trying to explain that they couldn't have our stuff because we needed it.

I began to make a long investigation of the problems—GCSE maths and physics, combined with problem-solving skills and a determination born out of having no other options, took the place of having any serious skills as a mechanic. Two hours later, and in discussion with the others, I had worked out what had happened. About three days earlier the steering had taken a particularly brutal knock as we slipped from a two-foot high sand rut. Afterwards, Chloe and I had noticed that the steering was very loose at one point in the turning circle: it was possible to turn the steering wheel almost ninety degrees with no corresponding movement in the road wheels. We had noted it down as something to look at in Kananga, assuming that it was just loose and needed tightening up.

What had actually happened was that the fall had knocked a chunk out of the spiral in the steering box that guided the roller which turned the wheels. Our accident had actually been caused by the fragment getting jammed between the roller and the spiral, thus locking the steering. This in turn had led the system to over-pressurise causing the pipe to burst. Chloe had not actually driven into a tree: 9Bob had. The real question was how we were going to fix it, but by this point it was getting dark and so we went to bed, making camp on the track. Eventually the crowd drifted away, as night was approaching.

The next day we awoke early and worked all morning on 9Bob. Chloe used her best doctor's plastering technique, chemical metal and crepe bandage, and repaired the pipe. Sucking the ATF carefully from the steering box (with a syringe begged from Chloe's med kit) I managed to fish the piece out with a magnet, reassemble the box and re-pressurise the system. We had about a litre of ATF left, the bottle having become dislodged and leaking in the jolting. It was used in the gearbox, too, which had already leaked since leaving Kinshasa. In context, the capacity of both the power steering and gear systems was about five or six litres. The steering wasn't great—it still had the non-responsive section, but it would do—Kananga was only a day away. We were painfully aware that 9Bob was a very old car, and it was a testament to Land Rover that he was still going at all, let alone driving across the Congo.

It was hot, greasy work and as we sweated, the heat rose above us and seemed to stay, trapped by the overarching trees from both sides of the narrow track that met above us. The thirty or more onlookers crowded alongside the car added to the sense of claustrophobia and entrapment. We were relieved to get moving again, to feel a breeze of fresh air, and looking forward to maybe finding a stream to wash in. Waving goodbye to the crowd, who by this time had cleared a space in the jungle adjacent to the car to watch us better, we drove fourteen miles that evening.

We found a delightful spot in a small clearing in the jungle, by the side of the road and 150 yards away from a stream. It was one of the nicest camping spots that we stayed at. The stream even had a relatively new, military-type metal bridge from which people had gradually been stealing bits. It was now in such a condition that if any more bolts were stolen it would cease to be a bridge: in other words, the next piece of looting from a communal asset would stop that individual thief from using the bridge and so the looting had stopped at that point, but not before. It was a story of the Congo that we contemplated as we washed. We had a fire and cooked a big bean stew, treating ourselves to a tin of sardines. We finished off our gin. We were happy. One day to go to Kananga!

The next morning Charlie did the usual vehicle checks and noticed some seepage of fluid from the power steering system. What we should have done was to ignore it and to try and limp to Kananga. But what we did was try to fix it, as we were critically low on ATF and couldn't afford any losses. As the mechanic this was my decision, and it was the wrong one. Two days, a cannibalised camp chair, broken jubilee clips, cut pipes, stretched tubing and nearly all our epoxy resin later, we admitted defeat.

We were stuck. And our prison, while still idyllic, had become a little strange. We seemed to be 'parked' in-between two different villages each with a large population of children. They enjoyed out-competing each other shouting 'GOOD MORNING TEACHER' at us; sometimes fights would ensue and occasionally it would get out of hand. It was pretty hard for us to fix the steering box whilst managing fifty children and stopping them from stealing our stuff. Once or twice we even had to go up to the village and get one of the adults to come down and discipline the children, but that only had a temporary effect.

On the second day, a policeman in full uniform arrived with the English teacher and demanded to know why we were here, as if we had chosen to stay. To be fair to him, it was utterly bizarre that we were there.

'You must leave immediately,' he said.

It took us a while to realise that we were in a massive diamond mining area—later we saw rich villages with motorbikes and satellite receivers run by generators. Every morning we would see young men walk past with sifting pans and shovels. Occasionally a Hilux would pass, carrying palm oil and people in the back and a diamond dealer in the front seat. When we washed in the stream we looked carefully at the bottom for sparkles. Our presence clearly made the policeman nervous. But neither of us had a choice: 9Bob wasn't moving and that was that. He left, but not before ordering the local village chief to sit with us until we departed. The chief didn't look very happy, but we gave him our surviving chair, a cup of tea and a packet of cigarettes. He perked up. It did, however, mean that the crowd was well behaved for a while.

There was a constant stream of interesting people on this path—students doing their examinations who were carrying guinea pigs to give to their teachers and with compulsory travel passes around their necks; polio caseworkers on foot going to investigate suspected infections; and travelling merchants pushing their heavily laden bikes. It was impressive how much of the state's machinery existed here, perhaps a result of our proximity to the provincial centre. There were also women walking to the fields and troops of children carrying buckets, bowls and cups of water back to the village. One night a chanting funeral procession marched past us in wailing grief, the sounds of their chants interrupted by sobs. We stood respectfully and watched them disappear into the black.

We had come to the conclusion that the only way out of our predicament was to split the party and for me to head to Kananga on my own to try to get a new steering box and ATF pipe. I started packing my bag, and Chloe drew the steering box, marking down all of the identification letters. Once I had left we would have had no way of communicating (our satellite phone had been long broken by this point), and so we discussed contingency plans.

In short, if I hadn't returned by midday on the seventh day, the other two were to make plans to follow me to Kananga the next morning, taking as many items of portable wealth as possible with them. Ideally they were to try and arrange some sort of police and/or village protection for 9Bob, but no-one really thought that there would be much left of the vehicle once we had abandoned it in the middle of the *brousse*. I would leave messages on everyone's email accounts and would plan to stay at the Catholic mission in Kananga. Finally, I took a GPS fix, swung my pack onto my back and walked up the path. Before I left I insisted that Charlie promise not to let Chloe out of his sight, even for five seconds.

My original plan was to get a motorbike back to the Route Nationale and then to try to hitch or buy a lift on a rut-making lorry to Kananga. The first part of the plan failed because the people in the village saw an opportunity and wanted to charge me $50 for a twenty-minute motorbike ride. I started walking. After passing through several villages, where the prices ranged from the sublime to the ridiculous, someone finally offered me a ride for a sensible price. It was not just a question of not wishing to be ripped off. I only had a limited amount of money and needed to buy a steering box, for which I could be charged anything.

The motorbike ride was short and took me to a town called Kilembe at the junction of the track and the Route Nationale. The bike didn't go straight to the main road, but first passed by a row of men seated with digital scales in front of them. The driver stopped and said that he would wait while I spoke to the men. I looked at him incredulously, and said some sharper words than were probably necessary. By this point I hadn't washed for several days and was covered in engine oil, dirt and grime. I was desperate to complete my mission and get back to the team, but as far as the locals were concerned, I was there for diamonds. There was simply no other reason for three *mondele* to be in the area.

With some further gentle prodding the driver was persuaded to take me to the main road, where he dropped me off inside a small food shack. Again, no-one was willing to sell me anything to eat or drink at reasonable prices, so I waited for a truck. After several hours I was still waiting, still explaining to everyone why I was there. Eventually the locals got bored and left me alone and a kind women gave me some water and soap so that I would wash myself in the village's ablutions hut. By now it was starting to get dark and the food shack became deserted. Still no lorry. I dozed fitfully on a wooden bench, trying not to sleep too deeply in case I missed my ride.

Meanwhile, Chloe and Charlie were having more success. There was a list of jobs to be done on the car (there always was), including extracting the old steering box. In the expectation that they might be there for some time they also dug a latrine hole and built a fire pit. They cleaned the vehicle, did an inventory of what food was left and learned to wash their clothes in the river using the cobs left from maize. The women taught Chloe to cook cassava leaves and plantain, and they negotiated for papayas that the children found in the jungle. They bought sugarcane from passing children (Charlie was an absolute addict) and checked daily on the health of a man passing to get his malaria treatment from the local clinic. They spent hours trying to explain to the same people why they could not afford to give away the contents of the car.

They broke up fights between the children, obliged when asked for photographs and dodged stones thrown at *les blancs* by some bigger children from a village a little further away. Sometimes the children sat quietly watching them while picking the lice from each other's heads, sporadically shouting *mondele, mondele* to get their attention. *Mondele* means white man in Lingala, but is derived from a term implying insincerity and can also be used to refer to zombies. It rang in our ears day after day. On one occasion, a man ran out of the jungle, ripped out a handful of Chloe's hair and ran off. The laughing crowd swore ignorance, but one later told us that it was for a black magic spell. Chloe was shaken, conscious of her vulnerability. The only times to relax were the evenings spent by the fire, as the crowd always dissipated when darkness came. It had only been a week since leaving Kinshasa, but it felt like a lifetime ago.

One day they locked up the car and accepted an invitation to the nearest village, surprised and touched by the hospitality. On the Muslim side of the track they shared a saltfish and cassava lunch served to them by a young man in a Star Trek uniform. Everywhere people were dressed in first-world cast-offs collected in Europe by various charities and then cynically sold at travelling jungle markets rather than given to the population. This resulted in people walking around with clothes on that were often either inappropriate—a grandmother, say, with a t-shirt that said 'Squeeze Me' or 'Fit Body Inside'— or utterly parochial: 'Dave's Prague Stag Tour, 1997'. You simply didn't know what to think, there were so many layers of meaning surrounding what they were wearing.

They also tried hard to get in contact with me. To achieve this they had to visit another village where there was a point of network signal, marked by a stick in the ground. The Community Health Officer showed them how to tie their phones to a long bamboo cane, set the text message up to send, and then raise the phone on the stick immediately after pressing send. It was hard to know how long to wait for a reply, but when the screaming from a young woman outside the clinic having dressing changes on deep ulcers on her leg became unbearable, they returned to the clearing. Moving through villages like a bizarre procession with a dust-raising cacophony of children, proud to accompany the only *blancs* they'd ever seen, was a pleasant relief from working on the car.

Meanwhile, my lorry arrived at six the next morning. It was a fuel lorry with 20,000 litres of diesel and petrol in plastic cooking oil containers. Arriving on or in the lorry were a random assortment of people who were to become my travelling companions over the next day. In the cab was the owner of the lorry with two middle-class ladies who were travelling from Kinshasa to visit their families in Kananga. As this was the Congo, sitting in the cab was considered luxury public transport.

On the top of the lorry, where I travelled, was a motley crew. Jean-Claude, the pastor. Marie, a rotund woman, who, judging by her later advances, was a part-time prostitute. Others, whose names I have forgotten, provided a spectacle as the journey progressed. Lastly, two young lads, who must have been about seventeen, worked as vehicle crew, digging it out when it got stuck. Their job for much of the journey was to go in front of the lorry and lay down long bits of timber to give the wheels grip in the terribly deep sand. Once the lorry had passed, they had to dig the spars out of the sand and run to the front to lay them down again. It looked utterly exhausting and I felt terribly sorry for them.

I sauntered over to the cab and asked for a ride. '$100' was the response (the actual price was $10, I had found out through some previous intelligence gathering). By this point, without much sleep, I was beginning to lose my temper, but I simply laughed and pointed at my ripped and oily clothes, playing the Congolese at their own game. 'Do you think I have $100? I don't even have enough to eat.' The lady from the teashop where I had 'slept' joined in as well. 'It's true, he hasn't eaten for a day.' The crew from the top of the truck peered down at the weird specimen. I was allowed on for $10.

It was a strange journey. The lorry moved at walking pace pretty much the entire way. It leaned from side to side violently as the wheels fell into ruts. This necessitated all those on the top of the lorry tying themselves down to stop them falling to what would almost certainly be serious injury or death. It was not comfortable, and there were only a few places where it was possible to rest without a jerry can sticking in the small of your back. These places were allotted through physical showdown with your neighbours. I often woke up to find that my neighbour had rolled me out of where I was sleeping and that I was precariously balanced, only held on by the ropes that I had wrapped around my torso. I then had to re-create my sleeping space through physically moving other people out of the way. At first I had naively asked for space and the others had just laughed at me. There was no malice in it, it was just the way things were in the Congo. We constantly smoked rough Congolese cigarettes despite being sat on a petrol bomb.

The monotony was broken by arrival into various villages along the route. The lorry would immediately be mobbed by everyone in the village, some selling bananas or peanuts or coffee, some running and shouting. Sometimes for entertainment, my companions would shout obscenities at villagers and sometimes they would shout back. It was bizarre. Jean-Claude seemed to know the route quite well and pointed out the different villages' attributes. It was a complete smorgasbord: some Muslim, some Christian, some animist (he liked those ones as he saw them as potential future clients). Some spoke various dialects of Tshiluba, some Kituba, some Lingala. It was complete linguistic chaos: there are over 215 languages spoken in the DRC.

'How do these people interact?' I asked.

'Sometimes an educated villager will speak a couple of languages, or they might use basic French or Lingala; but sometimes they just don't communicate,' came the answer from Jean-Claude. I found it a profoundly unsatisfying response: how was this country meant to function?

This truck journey was the first time I had been alone with my thoughts for a long time. I could no longer avoid it; I had to be honest with myself. Did I want to spend the rest of my life with Chloe? Framed like that, and despite Chloe being an amazing woman whom I still deeply respect, the answer was no. We had both been unhappy for some time in the relationship, and we were only just realising it. In the middle of the Congo I took a unilateral decision about our joint endeavour. In retrospect, it was completely unfair on Chloe to do so (even if the outcome would have been the same in the end) and we should have continued discussing it together. But once the decision was made, rightly or wrongly, I felt relieved.

Eventually the truck rumbled into Kananga at eight the next morning. It was a very run-down colonial town, with wide boulevards that gave the impression of a spaghetti western film set. The central market road was tarmacked but slightly potholed. I hired a motorbike and a driver called Padi for the day. Previously he had been one of the poor souls who worked transporting goods on a pushbike to take advantage of price differences between the towns and villages—the *velo* boys. Typically the bikes were adapted with a wooden pole pointing upwards bound to the seat post, and another to the handlebar post with which the bike would be held upright and against which the shoulder would brace. Usually the bikes were loaded with at least a hundred kilos of goods: beans, rice, palm oil. Occasionally a chicken or pig would be strapped on top or a pitifully bleating goat dragged behind.

Padi would sometimes be able to earn $70 for a four-day trip of pretty much non-stop pushing of a laden bike through sand. It was a desperate way to earn a living, but it marked him out as a high earner in this part of the Congo. The only people who had the potential to earn more were the artisanal diamond miners, but they relied on luck and their village being near a diamond seam.

If someone worked a seam that was not theirs they would be killed. Through this backbreaking work Padi had saved enough to buy a motorbike, and he now earned his living in a manner more befitting of his thirty years—most of the *velo* boys were in their early twenties; you had to be in your physical prime to cope with the work. Life expectancy in the DRC is forty-nine years; Padi was practically retired.

We set off on his bike together, first to go to the spare parts section of the market. I did not hold out much hope—I needed to find a steering box for a particular model of Land Rover in a part of the world where everyone had Toyota Land Cruisers. I expected that I would have to order it in the UK and get it couriered out to me; but even whether that was possible I did not know. The presence of the regional headquarters of the UN with its various agencies was a good sign, though. The market didn't produce anything, but the stallholders offered to make some investigations. They felt slightly sorry for me and sat me down with a coffee and some fried dough balls while they made some calls. It quickly became apparent that the car trade in Kananga was sewn up by the Muslim section of the population and they all knew each other. Luckily they seemed to have taken me under their wing.

'Try so-and-so, he's got an old Land Rover on his drive.' Off we went. Unbelievable. It was exactly the same model. This had been a lot easier than expected. After chatting to the owner briefly, I went across and began to test the steering box. It had exactly the same fault in it as the one in 9Bob—part of the spiral had been knocked out by the incredibly unforgiving terrain. It was hard to know who was more disappointed—the owner who had probably just missed out on several months' worth of income, or me, who might still have to abandon 9Bob in the bush.

Padi next took me round a series of car dealerships and car scrapyards. Would a Toyota box fit? Could they put a new spiral in? Various options were debated and dismissed. By this point, the whole network was buzzing with the news of *le blanc* who was trying to buy some obscure car part. 'How about Monsieur Land Rover?' said one of the dealers. Padi didn't know Monsieur Land Rover, but it sounded very promising. It was a place right on the edge of town, some distance away, but we went straight away. It was a Land Rover graveyard.

Containing my excitement, I inspected all the vehicles. Immediately I dismissed all those with the steering wheels on the wrong side; also some others that didn't have steering boxes—it was obviously a common problem here. Ultimately I was left with one option: a fairly new, bright white, EU-donated Land Rover that had a cluster of Congolese men gathered round and working on it. They all looked at me, instantly read the situation and smiled.

'So, are you selling any bits of that Land Rover?' I asked gently.

'Sure' was the response, 'which bit do you want?' 'Just the steering box,' I said, as I explained some of the story, but not enough for them to realise how desperate we were.

'$1000,' came the response. Ahhhhh!

We desperately needed that box. I politely ignored the offer and changed the subject, trying to get the story of the vehicle. Apparently it had only arrived in Kananga three years ago and had been donated to the governorship by the EU. It was now being sold for scrap. The problem was that it had been delivered without any spare parts. The roads around here were so punishing that its owners had only managed to keep it on the road for a short time, and even then it had been a struggle trying to cobble together repairs. Eventually something had broken that was not available and not replaceable with a jury-rig, and the Land Rover became the end point for most of the development aid that we were to see in the Congo—broken, stolen, sold off, wasted. I was determined, though, that at least three UK taxpayers were going to see benefit from this sorry wreck.

Turning back to the negotiation and not wishing to have a breakdown in communication or to box myself into a corner by negotiating too hard, I said that it was a real shame. I *really* wanted to buy the box from them but I simply didn't have that much money. In any case, I continued, I could order it on the internet and have it delivered here from England in three days and it would only cost $500. I could stay in the church for free and so it was just my time that was being spent. I was lying through my teeth. Amazingly, this complete bluff worked and they settled on $650. There were still issues—I only had $600 in cash and there were many other things to buy, but the main problem was solved. What a complete stroke of luck. We shook on it and agreed to meet in a couple of hours once the mechanics had removed the box and I had got the money together.

Padi drove me to a bank in the centre of town. Inside was a rugby scrum of activity. There was no ATM and I began to queue so that I could take money out on my card. At the front of the queue was a middle-aged white woman shouting to make herself heard. She was trying to cash a cheque. People were pushing past her and in front of her and completely disrupting her transaction. It really was a free-for-all. At last I got to the front of the queue and found out that they had never seen a Visa or MasterCard before. This was a setback.

'What's the problem?' asked the white woman. I explained. 'I'll lend you the money, how much do you need?'

I couldn't believe it: she hadn't even asked how we were going to pay her back and she had offered help. Ruth was an American missionary on a long-term education project. She was just coming to the end of a two-year stint and was about to head home for some holiday. What a kind woman. We left the bank, talking about Ruth's project. She was trying to reverse the local legacy of the 'civilising' project of Church missionaries in the 1800s. The insistence on marriage by the Church had meant that when men died widows were sometimes left destitute if their husband's family came to appropriate the couple's property after the funeral. Previously, according to Ruth, the tribal arrangements had meant that the women were cared for in the community and were allowed to keep the joint property. Of course, in (for example) European Christian societies this situation would be covered by wills and testaments, but these did not really exist in the Congo. It was a fascinating legacy of colonialism.

We walked together to Ruth's apartment and she gave me a few hundred dollars. I arranged to have my aunt in America pay Ruth back into her US account. My father in the UK would pay the aunt back and I would pay my father back. In the event, these arrangements were slightly delayed when my father assumed that the email he was receiving from the Congo asking for money, supposedly from his son, was a scam! But it really couldn't have gone any better. I went back to buy the box, then went to the market to get the pipe

welded and pick up several litres of ATF for the steering system. I also had a short list of other spare parts that we needed. Padi and I ate, and he agreed to drive me back to the rest of the party *dans la brousse*. By a massive stroke of luck I had completed all the errands in eight hours.

The ride back was relatively uneventful except for a nasty run-in with some demanding officials as we were leaving Kananga. Padi went to pay a bribe and I stopped him, as per the trip's policy. Padi looked at me in horror and said, 'What are you doing? We either pay now, or they get me later.' Padi's obvious subtext was asking me why I was causing him these problems. Did I not understand how the Congo worked? So Padi paid the bribe, equivalent to $3, and I later (reluctantly) reimbursed him. It was the only bribe that was indirectly paid by the team in the Congo.

Padi's motorbike meant that it was easier to leave the Route Nationale and weave our way through the villages at a faster speed. I left the GPS on track mode so as to make it easier for us later to retrace the steps in 9Bob. We slept at a trucking stop and then carried on early in the morning. By eleven the team was reunited. It was the fourth day of my absence, and Charlie and

Chloe had settled down to some serious relaxing. Fairly typically, as I arrived on the back of Padi's bike tooting the horn and cheering, Chloe and Charlie stretched, yawned and rolled over on the mat. Jokingly they said, 'Couldn't you have stayed away a little longer? It was much more peaceful without you,' but in reality they had been feeling like they were in an open prison.

The remainder of the day was spent fitting the new steering box and further repairing the pipe that I had had welded in Kananga. As Chloe and I lay side by side in the mosquito dome that night, I told her that I was ending our relationship. I invited her to persuade me otherwise, but my mind was set. Although it was not exactly unexpected, the manner and timing of my decision broke something inside Chloe. In her heart of hearts she knew where our relationship was heading, but until this point we'd been a team no matter what. Now I had taken a decision that would change the course of her life. I regret not discussing it with her, though she understood that once I had made my mind up I had no choice but to tell her straight away. Carrying on in falsehood would have made it even worse. It was a long night for both of us, and I don't think Chloe slept at all.

A day later, eight days after arriving in the jungle clearing, we got up early, did the daily vehicle checks, prepared the breakfast and struck camp. I took Charlie to one side and told him what had happened the night before. He nodded, patted me on the arm and said, 'all right, mate'. He then did the best thing that he could have done and carried on just the same towards both of us, which can't have been an easy balance. Our departure was sweetened by a bunch of bananas given to us by the local English teacher—a touching gesture of hospitality. Mixing the mundane with the profound, we also filled in the latrine lest some small child fall into it. Thankfully there was no leaking from the steering system and we were able to continue. There was silence in the car that morning and guilt started to eat at me.

That day we covered 125 miles, crisscrossing the Route Nationale No.1 and benefiting from the GPS log. The quality of the road varied between newly repaired and totally impassable. We got bogged in several times, but this was now becoming *de rigueur*. One of us would get out and put the tea on and talk to anyone who turned up, the other two would start digging, positioning waffle boards and/or driving forwards or backwards to get 9Bob out of the sand or off the compacted earth ridges.

Eventually, towards late afternoon, we drove into Kananga and were stopped at the checkpoint where I had previously had the trouble with Padi. The checkpoint was actually a toll booth. There had been several toll booths since Kinshasa, all charging relatively large amounts of money—as a four wheel drive our vehicle attracted the maximum toll, probably because the only people who could afford four wheel drives in the DRC were as rich as Croesus. As we progressed from Kinshasa we had become progressively more annoyed at paying the toll because there hadn't really been a road. Now the road had broken our car and the government still wanted to charge us. Through gritted teeth we paid.

Getting to Kananga was a relief and we went straight to the Catholic mission to ask for a place to spend a couple of days. We were exhausted and emotionally drained. It had been a struggle to complete what we thought would have been the easiest part of the trip—originally we had been told at the British embassy that the road was tarmacked all the way to Kananga from Kinshasa, but one supposes that they had never driven it. My legs were covered in badly infected cuts and bites and I had a low-grade fever. As Chloe carefully cleaned and dressed them I almost fainted from the pain and exhaustion.

We were given a room with a bed to sleep in, and leftover bottles and tissues from the previous guest. The gold-adorned head priest clearly thought we were richer than we were and tried to charge us several hundred dollars for the pleasure. Chloe, who was handling the negotiations for the room, patiently bargained him down, pointing out that we were still washing out of an oil drum, and that no meals were included. He demurred and they finally settled on $30 a night. The three of us crept out for a beer and some goat and *chikwanga* (a gelatinous substance made from fermented cassava cooked in banana leaves).

We slept soundly.

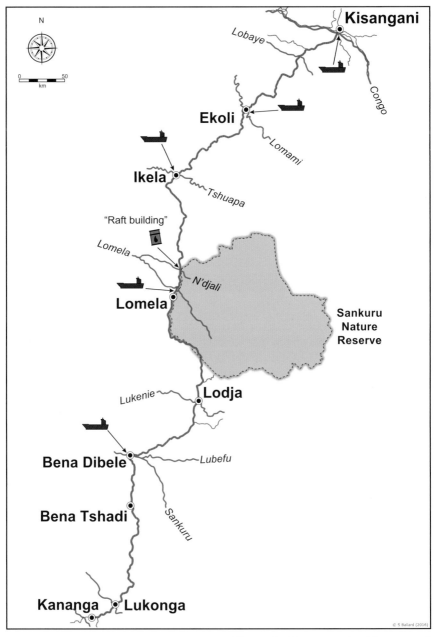

Stage 2: Kananga to Kisangani

Chapter 3
Kananga to Lomela

Day 28-9: Kananga - 14 miles
Day 30: Kananga to north of Kapambue - 63 miles
Day 31: North of Kapambue to north of Bena Tshadi - 83 miles
Day 32: North of Bena Tshadi to Okayakole - 69 miles
Day 33: Okayakole to Lodja - 68 miles
Day 34: Lodja to 15 miles north of Lodja- 24 miles
Day 35: North of Lodja to Lomela - 110 miles

We spent three days in Kananga, working on the car and re-stocking it. We fixed the leaking back axle/hub and pre-emptively changed the universal joints on the front prop-shaft, aware that this was 9Bob's weakest area to date. We were keen to strengthen the car for the road ahead. As with all of our part replacement decisions, they either turned out to be a stroke of genius or a nightmare—there seemed to be little in-between. In this case it was the latter. We couldn't reassemble the joint, lost some of the pins and could not find a replacement. The three of us spent a whole day working on one joint and traipsing around town followed by a dishevelled madman who would turn up and start talking to us in gibberish. It wasn't that he wasn't speaking French and so we couldn't understand him: no-one else could either.

Chloe and I briefly discussed whether to abort the trip, but decided that irrespective of emotional developments we wanted to complete what we had started. Anyway we would have had to abandon 9Bob, which neither of us wanted to do.

We tried to gather information about our route. The provincial police laughed at us as if we were mad. They could only tell us about the first seventy miles or so—their jurisdiction. There was also a UN headquarters in the

town, but the people there refused to talk to us. We spent some time trying to find some lorry drivers who had done the route, but the route, we were told, was only big enough for cars. No trucks going north. Looking at the map, we could see that there were five rivers to cross. We knew after the previous fortnight that the Land Rover could cope with pretty much any terrain, but we also knew that a river without a way to cross it would stop us dead and force us to retrace our steps. Little pictures of barges on the map indicated that none of the rivers had functional bridges.

There was another option by way of a north–south route in the east of the country, but this was the scene of heavy fighting between UN forces and various rebel groups. We didn't fancy our chances in a British-plated Land Rover. So in the end we decided to take the first route, up the centre of the country with its five river crossings. There were, we reasoned, and according to the map at least, several branch roads. If there was no way to cross a river we would cut across to the east and take our chances with the rebels. The one thing we were not going to do, unless we absolutely had to, was give up. In any case, what would we do with the vehicle? Unless we drove him out we would have to abandon him at quite some financial cost. No. We were going to complete the trip.

The town of Kananga itself was strange. There was a huge train station, at which trains would arrive from the south once a week. The rest of the week there was a market on the tracks that moved off just in time for the train's arrival. The paved streets were clean and wide but there were no phone lines, no running water and, as previously described, no banking system. We were worried about how much cash we had and so we changed everything into Congolese francs except for our emergency reserve (people mostly only accepted francs in the bush). It took over two hours to change a few hundred euros and dollars as the bank clerks examined each note, rejecting those with creases.

The mostly empty shelves of the only 'supermarket' in town contained only spirits and Quaker Oats. We tried to get on the internet to reassure our families that we were ok, but it was slow going. On our final night we found a bar in a tumbledown old colonial building that had been, we think, the bakery. As we sipped our beers by torchlight on the rickety veranda it felt very much like post-civilisation living.

We set off after a lie-in and drove along the well-made road towards Muji Mayo. There was the ubiquitous checkpoint. The police were slightly confused as to why we would want to go to Kisangani, or even how we were going to get there, but they let us through with the usual formalities and the payment of an official toll fee. We all remember this checkpoint because of the cruelty being inflicted at it: a monkey was kept by a chain wrapped around his neck and tied to a tree in such a way that it could either stand on a branch or hang with its paws not touching the ground. Every time he tried to climb up onto the limb, a child would hit the monkey on the head, knocking it off its perch. He would then proceed to hit the monkey from side to side. Three or four other people watched on, bored. We became fairly used to this sort of casual cruelty during the trip, but it was always unpleasant to witness.

Back on the road and shortly before the town, there was an unmarked track to the left. Apparently this was the road between two of the major cities in the country. We stopped at the junction and asked some villagers, 'Is this the route to Kisangani?' (750 miles away)

'No.'

'How about Lodja?' (250 miles away)

'No.'

Charlie went and got the small scale map, and asked, 'Is this the route to Lukonga?'—a town that was about two miles down the road.

The villager thought for a moment and nodded his head. We were off!

We left the rolling green hills and orange groves around Kananga and re-entered the rainforest. The route was actually in fairly good condition, like a large rabbit run with the trees coming together over the top. It would probably be described as a 'passable 4x4 track' in an off-road travel guide, protected by the fact that it was too small for lorries. Though intermittent holes and poo were still features, the villagers were much friendlier and more helpful with directions. Through later studying the Second Congo War we

realised that this area had not experienced as much fighting as other areas, probably because it didn't have any natural resources.

As we had when we left Kinshasa, we saw NGO billboards by the side of the road advertising their projects, with some funded by DFID, the UK's development agency. These included one or two complete clinics, which seemed like a good use of money. We managed to cover sixty-three miles that day and camped by the side of the road with a fire. One notable feature of this section of the journey was the hatching butterflies that had escaped the caterpillar farms (a national food staple). They would all hatch at once and cloud around in their thousands creating a beautiful effect. They would also frequently settle on our sweaty skin whenever we were still, probing for moisture. That night Charlie gave Chloe and me some space so that we could talk. Chloe asked me to explain myself again, which I did as best I could.

The next morning a mist had descended over the area through which we could just see the sun rising. It was breathtakingly beautiful and Charlie took photos of some girls walking out of the mist with the sun rising behind them. It seemed a shame to leave but we wanted to try to get to our first river crossing that day. The roads were wide and relatively compact and we made good time, until we hit a police roadblock—or more accurately a trackblock. This was strange, as normally the police would not be manning roadblocks this far out of town. I, easily the most impatient member of the team, hoped that this wouldn't become the norm for the next leg of our journey.

An old police chief with a pleasant face ambled over and asked us what we were doing here. Chloe explained and he nodded sagely. We asked him why there was a roadblock with several policemen with riot shields standing beside it. 'Well, you see,' he said, 'these two villages here'—pointing at the jungle in front of us and behind us—'are at war at the moment.' He explained further that there had been a long-running dispute over some land that both the villages claimed. Over the last few weeks tensions had risen and there had been a series of raids and fights. At the moment the police had been told to hold the line while the governor was sent for to resolve the dispute. He didn't think there would be any problems with us continuing, so we bought some fried plantain snacks and set off again.

It was to be a day of strange meetings. Some distance later, by the side of the road and heading in the opposite direction, was a muddy white Land Rover. It was the only car we had seen since leaving the main Kananga-Muji Mayo road, and the first Land Rover since Kinshasa. Its owners had the hood up and were tinkering with something while another man was working on the wheel hubs. We stopped and found out that they were examiners who were travelling from school to school with end-of-year exam papers for the students.

We were amazed that these parts of the state still worked, even though it was clear in this case that it was in large part due to the dedication of the individuals rather than the beneficence of the ministry—here, an examiner was on his knees in the dirt trying to repair Land Rover wheel hubs. Thankfully, we could help—we had a box of wheel bearings and were able to donate enough to get them back on the road. The examiner was very grateful but also very angry. 'They steal everything in the ministry,' he said, 'so we have nothing down here. I know the foreigners are giving lots of money to the government here, I hear it on the news, but none of it makes it to the district level. This is how we used to examine during the war.' His tirade over, he finished with, 'If you ever meet the president, tell him how much we are suffering.'

This proud man's complaints chimed with conversations we'd had with educated Congolese elsewhere in West Africa and with what we'd read (Trefon 2011). Kabila's government had advertised its *cinq chantiers* (five pillars) programme for the elections—infrastructure, health and education, water and electricity, housing and employment—and the Congolese joke that their struggle to survive is the *sixième chantier* (sixth pillar). They understand perfectly that their president and his close inner circle are legitimised and sustained by their receipt of international aid and that they use it to accumulate further wealth at the expense of the people. The response of the population is bitterness combined with resignation, and we were depressed at western complicity in the charade. That said, I understood from my previous work in Afghanistan that western ignorance was just that—ignorance—rather than some grand plot to keep the Congo poor. Western governments and aid programmes were just a lot more stupid than they looked, though the Congolese had other suspicions.

As we neared our first crossing point to the north of Bena Tshadi, we were surprised to see a large Belgian road sign at a fork in the road. By the junction there were also a couple of dilapidated brick buildings. Getting out we also noticed—amazingly—that there were scraps of tarmac under our feet. It was like uncovering an ancient civilisation: littered all around were engine blocks and vehicle chassis used as animal pens, and peering further into the jungle we could make out outlines of bits of buildings that had half fallen down. Bena Tshadi had once been the district administrative centre during the Belgian era. It was fascinating. It was only fifty years ago that the Belgians left, and although people still lived here the jungle was reclaiming all that was unused.

The old road to the crossing point had already been subsumed by vegetation and there was another track down to the river. We were never going to make it that night—it was already late afternoon. We bedded down for the night to the side of the narrow jungle track down to the river. That evening, while working on the engine, I managed to crack a valve on the vacuum pump for the brake system: these were the perils of my amateurism. Despite some herculean team efforts with glue, coat hangers and rubber tubing, we could not fix it. We still had brakes but they were a lot less effective without the vacuum; 9Bob was severely overladen and this greatly increased our stopping distances. It was a good job, Charlie joked, that we were never able to go that fast.

The following morning we did not have far to go to get to the crossing point. As the vegetation broke we entered a massive flat sand area. There was the usual checkpoint manned by some people in shorts and t-shirts. We pushed on to the water's edge where there was a collection of pirogues—long, narrow canoes carved out of single tree trunks—the equivalent of water taxis. On the far bank about 400 yards away was a boat that looked like a two-car ferry. A quick game of paper-scissors-stone decided that the other two would cross and try to get the boat to pick us up. I would stay with the vehicle, which was predictably generating a lot of interest from the fishermen. Before approaching the pirogues Chloe and Charlie checked the price for passage with the assembled crowd—it was 100 francs for locals, 200 francs for motorbikes or foreigners. The canoe-man immediately demanded

1000 francs when they approached, inflating the price ten-fold and holding his nerve until they recruited the crowd to back them up. Charlie started the negotiations with aplomb.

'I need to speak with my brother, the barge captain. We are brother professionals.'

He then proceeded to spin a yarn about how he was a boat captain in England and was on holiday with his friends to see the barges of the Congo. This, before they had even been offered a price! With this gambit, a further half hour of negotiating/begging and through involving the local big man, 'Papa Joseph', as a mediator, Chloe and Charlie managed to get the price down to around $60. This was a good effort considering that they had us over a barrel. Later we realised that we would have to repeat this at each of the four remaining crossings, and that our problem would probably not be that there was no way to cross, but that they would be able to charge us what they liked when we got there.

Eventually a boy ran off with our money to buy the diesel and hydraulic oil necessary to make the boat run. Soon I was able, from the other bank, to discern some smoke from the engine, and finally the barge started to move with the engine boys dripping hydraulic fluid into the leaking engine as it went. Seeing that it was not going to land where I was, I moved the vehicle further up the river bank and managed to beach it on a sand dune. I quickly started digging and when the barge landed the others also sprinted to help—the engine could only run so long with the fuel and hydraulic fluid we'd paid for. Even Papa Joseph grabbed a shovel and helped digging.

Once on the other side we took stock and found some dough balls and plantain for lunch. Charlie bought himself a cup of coffee which he pronounced 'excellent' despite being cold (the Congolese grow their own coffee and so real coffee can be drunk—unlike in most of the rest of Africa where Nescafé is the norm). Amusingly, it caused a bout of projectile vomiting and fever later that day. I just laughed at him as he clutched his stomach while Chloe looked concerned. We couldn't afford this to be serious. Our bodies were really being put through their paces—all of us were losing weight and

all of us had something or the other wrong with us. Chloe ran a mini-surgery most evenings once we had stopped for the day. We pushed on looking for a spot to stay the night but didn't get very far before we came across a medium-sized lorry that was completely embedded in the road blocking our path. As we pulled up, the twenty-or-so passengers were trying heroically to push the lorry up a sandy slope in order to jump start the engine (they were travelling without an alternator or another lorry to restart them). We found out later that they had been there for forty-eight hours without food.

We looked to see what we could do to help. We had a spare battery but it simply wasn't big enough to turn the lorry's engine over. The obvious option was to try to jump start them, but we couldn't find long enough leads to get from the front of the lorry, along its length, to the front of 9Bob. The lorry mechanic wanted to connect the chassis of the vehicles together with a metal bar and just connect the positive terminals (that is, using the bar to complete the circuit). Here we faced a dilemma—it might work: with 9Bob's engine running and revving we might be able to deliver enough charge to turn the other engine over. The problem was that I was not sure whether when the lorry engine kicked it might overload some of the electrics in 9Bob. I thought I had read somewhere that the battery acts as a kind of damper against voltage spikes in the electrical system, but wasn't really sure. In the end we had to refuse, citing risk to 9Bob, since much as we wanted to help them we wouldn't be going anywhere without our electrical system.

While this discussion was going on Chloe had worked out that we could just edge around the side of the lorry with some very precise driving. Having been doing this for nearly five months now, we had got it down to a fine art. Generally Chloe drove and I would stand in front of the vehicle and give careful directions using agreed hand signals. Sad as we were not to be able to help the lorry and its passengers, we pushed on. The road here was actually being built and strengthened, and in places it had been raised or dug in with embankments. Later on we were to come across a man who was working for the project and he was to help us immensely. That evening we put our hammocks up in a semi-cleared bit of jungle and a group of some thirty villagers came out and sat watching us until it was dark.

As we were such an interesting spectacle to the villagers, the darkness of night was the only time we had any privacy. Though their curiosity was understandable, the constant crowds, which accumulated rapidly even seemingly in the middle of nowhere, were exhausting. Often this meant that darkness was the only time that Chloe could go to the toilet unobserved, or that we could sit quietly without items in our possession being requested. On this night it was also the only way that we could discuss plans for our separation on returning home, and that Chloe could cry without an audience. We could never let her out of our sight during the day for fear of her vulnerability, but at least in the dark she could have some dignity.

The next morning was Congolese National Day. We motored uneventfully to Lodja, the administrative centre of Sankuru District. Almost as soon as we got into town we were set upon by the DGM—Direction Générale de Migration. Uniquely among the countries that we had all visited the DRC had an internal migration department whose job was to keep track of, and stop, the Congolese from moving about within their own country: an appalling remnant of Belgian rule. They did their best to stop us moving about as well, but we had specifically gone to the ministry in Kinshasa to check whether we were allowed to move about freely in the country. The answer was so assuredly given—we did not need permission to circulate—that we didn't ask for it in writing. That was a mistake.

Of all the government departments that we had to deal with, including migration, police, army, secret service, mayoralty, governorships etc., all of whom were competing with each other for our potential bribe money, the DGM was by far the most annoying because its personnel had such large paperwork demands. We never worked out what the cause was. Certainly they wanted bribe money, but it was more than that. It seemed that they were angered that we could—legally—move about the country freely and there was nothing they could do to stop us. Whether they had not received news of the recent law change from Kinshasa that foreigners only needed a valid tourist visa to travel in the country, or whether they had and felt that it threatened their power base, we do not know. They were parasitic and I, particularly amongst the group, found it a total affront.

This particular DGM man insisted that we tell him where we were staying, which we didn't know because we had just arrived. He also told us he was hungry, but then so were we. As we drove around town he followed us on the back of a motorbike. With him in his leather jacket and dark sunglasses, it looked like a scene from a bad South American spy movie. Every time we stopped he would pop up and ask us where we were staying. We were very tempted to leave the town, but we needed to fix the brake vacuum pump. We finally settled on a cheap hotel and sat down to a lunch of goat. Up popped Monsieur DGM, the first guy's boss. By this point in the trip I had been banned by the other two from talking to anyone from the DGM because I almost instantly lost my temper when I did so. Like many other DGM officials, this man told us that we did not have permission to travel and we would have to turn back. A long argument ensued, which we won, but he threatened that he would make our trip 'very difficult' and that he would speak to his colleagues further on and make problems for us.

The strain was beginning to show on all of us, but I was being particularly badly behaved. In retrospect I can see that I was suffering from our break-up, but I was projecting my negative emotions onto Congolese officials rather than onto Chloe and Charlie. This escalating debate was taking place in a restaurant with bamboo walls while the other diners looked on mouths agape. Several of them later apologised for the official's behaviour, while Chloe and Charlie later told me they were deeply embarrassed by my behaviour. The official finished by insisting that we pay him money for photocopying our forms, which I refused to do. At last he realised that he would get nothing out of us and left promising to return. We never saw him again and this represented a pattern that we would see again and again.

Officials who are used to dominating the local population expect to be able to do the same to outsiders when they pass through. When we refused and they insisted they lost face in front of the people from whom they habitually stole in the name of the law. There were two differences between us and the local population, however. Firstly, we had gone right to the top to find out what the actual legal position was and so could speak with authority. Secondly, there was nothing really that the officials could do to us—we were passing through and we had the protection of our embassy, albeit from

Kinshasa. The locals didn't know the law and were stuck living with these rapacious thugs, perpetuating the culture of predation cultivated in Mobutu's Zaire. We felt sorry for them.

After that ugly scene we walked around town trying to find someone who had a Land Rover. It would be pure luck finding a spare part. After a while someone pointed us in the direction of a Portuguese man called Carlos who dug wells for drinking water. Surprised, we went to Carlos' compound. His Congolese wife told us that he was out but to wait as he would be back soon. We didn't know much Portuguese between us, but what we knew we polished up to greet him.

Soon a Land Rover swung into the yard and a lean man of about forty-five with a sun-toughened face got out. Someone had already told him about our arrival and he rushed up to us welcoming us in French and greeting us like long-lost friends. He called something to his wife and she emerged, improbably, with two bottles of scotch. A whisky lover, I thought I had arrived in heaven. Here began one of our luckiest friendships. Like Power in Kinshasa, Carlos helped us beyond reason, beyond expectation. It was a nice reminder of the beauty of the human spirit. We explained our problem to Carlos.

'First, we will eat, and then I will call Alfred, he is a *moreno* [mixed descent: he had a Congolese mother and Belgian father]. He is a magician with Land Rovers.'

He then took us over to see some of the work that Alfred had done on his own vehicle, and although everything was completely jury-rigged with borrowed parts it appeared to have been done in a very professional manner, unlike the work that I had been 'practising' on poor 9Bob.

He served us the most amazing spread of food while he told us his story. As we thought, he had spent most of his life in Africa. He had a wife in Portugal and was a strict Jehovah's Witness. He also had children back in Portugal as well as the smiley baby girl Chloe was cuddling. His wife here was the daughter of a local chief and was relatively well educated. He was working for a business that sank concrete-lined wells in the surrounding villages, paid for through aid grants. He had been here for a couple of years. His Congolese colleague Chef Antoine, a jovial man in his fifties, and two fellow Jehovah's Witnesses, Benois and Kenso, joined us.

We began to describe where we had been (all the way from London!) and to discuss our future plans. Carlos shook his head. 'You can't,' he said, 'the bridge is down.' Our original fears had been realised. Which of the four remaining crossing points was it? Surely the next one at Lomela? We got our maps out just as Alfred arrived. We introduced ourselves and Carlos explained what we were trying to do.

'It's not the Lomela crossing, there is a boat there, but after that, crossing the N'djali river, the bridge is down; it has been for fifteen years.' We laughed. We had been asking people about our route for the last thousand miles and no-one had told us about a key bridge that had been down since the Second Congo War. It wasn't even one of the five crossing points that we had identified—on our maps it wasn't even clear that there was a river there because the N'djali marked the boundary between two provinces (and time zones). We then found out that the N'djali had been a frontline between the government and the RCD for a couple of years. The bridge had been destroyed and for some reason, despite it being critical infrastructure—its absence severed one of two north–south routes in the country—it had never been replaced. Not for the first time we wondered where international development efforts had been directed. This could be a problem. Land Rovers don't float.

Opening out the maps, we traced other routes going east. As well being less than ideal from a security point of view we found out that those crossing points also had the bridges knocked out. According to Carlos, a rebel group had tried to isolate Kasai Oriental province from the rest of the country to the north and the east, and no-one had bothered since to repair the bridges they had destroyed. By a process of reduction we ended up back at the N'djali crossing as the most likely contender. Alfred, it turned out, had recently been tasked to go to the crossing and take some photos for a road-building crew— eventually there was to be a bridge and road built through here. Because he was an engineer he was also able to draw us cross-sections of the river with approximate depths and points of fastest flow. There were actually two channels to cross and the biggest span was about sixty-five feet. The first channel had a bridge that needed repairing and strengthening to take 9Bob's weight but the second was open water, with the burnt spars of the previous bridge sticking forlornly out of the water. We pondered whether we could rebuild the second bridge.

As the evening wore on we drank more scotch and discussed the options. Alfred worked for an American contractor who was willing to lend us Alfred's engineering skills to get a temporary bridge built—at the price of $1500. For the first time we began to think that we might not make it, but then Alfred, who although keen to join us could see we would be unable to pay his boss' price, suggested that we build a raft instead. We stared at him, incredulous—it was easier than a bridge, but really? None of us knew how to build them beyond having messed around in lakes as Scouts or Army Cadets. Alfred laughed that off and suggested we base it around *fûts*: empty oil drums. None of us had any idea how to work out displacement or how to balance a very front-heavy Land Rover (because of the engine) in the water. How were we going to power it? Would the current sweep it away? How would we load 9Bob onto it and get him off? We sat late into the night planning. Carlos, Alfred and Chef Antoine egged us on. 'Nobody has crossed that river with a vehicle for fifteen years!' 'This will be fantastic!' We had nothing to lose, there was no other way we were going to get across that river, and we discussed various combinations of tree trunks and oil drums.

The next day we woke up early and began to prepare. We bought six oil drums, two axes and two of the largest wedge-shaped machetes we could find. We had great difficulty locating any rope but were finally sent to the *mondele* (white man) store, which actually turned out to be run by two Indian Gujarati brothers. Lodja was quite a cosmopolitan place. We bought all of their remaining rope. In another act of great kindness Carlos personally introduced us to the police colonel in the town. He thought the whole project was very amusing and offered his support. This support later turned out to be crucial.

Alfred also managed to fix our brake vacuum pump. He laughed when he saw the state of our engine, which had various bits held together with surgical tape. We then conducted our normal victualling of fuel and food. Carlos

invited us to his house for a final meal. As we were driving out his wife
loaded us with fragrant white flowers and he handed us some Jehovah's
Witness literature—'something to read in case you get bored'. Not wishing
to offend him after his great kindness, we took it seriously and thanked
him, saying we would look into it. Their kindness really had been inspiring.
We were able to drive about twenty miles before it was time to camp.

That night we found a hollowed-out road embankment and camped
inside it. The area had recently been cleared for cultivation with fire (that is,
slash and burn) and so there was lots of firewood. We were starting to worry
about our cooking gas reserves and were trying to cook with fire as much
as possible. In addition, our water purifier was also starting to leak, and we
had begun boiling a big casserole pan of water on the fire last thing at night
and leaving it to cool overnight. That night we mixed flour and water and
cooked delicious 'bread rocks' in the embers for our breakfast. We found that
because they were unleavened a fist-size piece of bread with peanut butter
would fill you up until the middle of the afternoon. All too quickly we ran
out of flour brought from Kinshasa, and couldn't find any more.

Surviving on porridge, rice, spaghetti, dried beans, tinned sardines and
tinned peas or tomato puree as a treat, we were all starting to get rather thin

with the heavy exercise and long days. Charlie and I particularly were losing muscle mass and beginning to look gaunt. Unlike in any of the other countries we'd visited, it was very difficult to buy food along the routes outside the towns because they were so scarcely travelled. On the rare occasions when something was available it was usually bush meat; monkey, squirrel, cat or pangolin (a cute, armadillo-like creature), which it is not sensible to eat. No-one bothered to collect the eggs from the chickens running around. Fried caterpillars were a welcome source of protein when we could find women cooking them. Occasionally we could buy cassava leaves, bananas or papaya, but fresh vegetables were also in short supply. Wars and looting had taught the Congolese that farming was futile, so the area was predominantly populated by subsistence-gatherers, rarely with excess food to sell. We were hungry a lot of the time.

We set off as normal the next day and had a relatively uneventful morning on good roads. This section of the route between Kisangani and Kananga had been upgraded slightly, although why the contractors were starting in the middle of the route without even first putting bridges across all the rivers remained a mystery. Towards the early afternoon we reached a cluster of houses on the south bank of the second of our five crossings. Once over the other side we had about twenty miles to go to get to the N'djali, which would

leave us time to do a reconnaissance and start work in the morning on the bridge (for the first river channel) and raft construction (for the second river channel). As we neared the ferry point we were greeted by scenes of dancing teenagers. They had just completed their exams and were celebrating with friends and family. It was such a happy sight. We saw the boat over the other side of the narrow river and waved it over in high spirits.

As the boat started moving over we could see the owners of some small stalls smiling, pointing at us and laughing. We wondered if we were about to be taken for a ride on the price of the boat. The grin on the coxswain's face as he tied up the boat confirmed our suspicions: '$100,' he said, for a sixty-five-foot river crossing on a boat drawn by men pulling it along cables. It didn't even require a motor. Wearily we began to argue following our normal pattern. First we would try to make a joke out of it (normally Charlie's role). Then we would try appealing to the individual's good side and involve other people in the crowd by asking them to comment on the fairness or otherwise of the price (this was Chloe's role). This rarely worked, as most of the crowds that we had around us were firmly of the belief that we were to be exploited remorselessly. Finally we would harden our attitude and refuse to pay, while at the same time demanding to be taken across (normally my role). Usually through a combination of these methods, and some role reversal, we would pay something resembling a fair price.

As this negotiation was going on a World Food Programme (WFP) Land Cruiser loaded to the gunnels with Plumpy'Nut drove up behind us. Plumpy'Nut is a fully nutritionally balanced gloop designed to be given in re-feeding programmes to starving children, refugees or people whose nutrition needs supporting. The Congolese driver got out and joined the argument on our side. 'You have to charge them a fair price,' he insisted. It turned out that in fact, since it was a government-owned boat, there was no fee for crossing, just a donation to the men pulling the cable. The boat owner/manager had by this point come across the river and tried to argue simultaneously that he owned the boat so could set the prices, that it was a government-owned boat and he'd lose his job if we refused to pay the fixed price. Welcome to the Congo, we thought!

Eventually we were allowed to pay what we thought was fair, and we paid exactly the same as the WFP driver, about $7. While we were crossing we had a conversation with him. 'The problem is,' he said, 'these people never meet foreigners, and all they hear about is the amount of money that they have, and how they give it away the whole time. They see you as a resource, not as human beings.'

While the confrontation had been happening on the south bank, a crowd had gathered watching us on the north bank. Slightly apart from the crowd stood a taller man in a bright white shirt tucked into tight white trousers, quietly watching. We thought nothing of it at the time—big crowds gathering to watch us were nothing out of the ordinary. Once we got to the other side I hopped off the boat straight away and walked up the bank to scout out the onwards route. Charlie settled our bill and Chloe drove the vehicle off the barge, quickly getting stopped from going any further by the crowd. After a while we managed to create a path through them and parked 9Bob at the beginning of the road. Charlie seemed to be having another argument about how much we were paying and Chloe went down to help him while I stayed with the vehicle. By now the crowd of about forty was milling around 9Bob and the WFP vehicle. Charlie and Chloe came back, having given the coxswain the money and leaving him shouting at them.

'The guy in the white shirt says that we have to stop here,' said Charlie as he came up to the vehicle.

'Who is he?'

'No idea.'

'Fuck him then, let's go.'

We still wanted to make it to the river by nightfall and had lost an hour arguing about the boat price. By now the crowd was really beginning to surge, so we jumped in 9Bob and pulled away. As we did so the crowd suddenly pounced on the WFP vehicle and blocked its path. Then they wrenched open its doors and started looting it. We were stunned. What was this place that we were in?

We had about a mile along a track until we got to the Lomela District centre. We had been in two minds about whether to register with the district chief. On the one hand, we were going to be in the district for a couple of days and we already had the support of the provincial police colonel who had asked us to check in with his subordinate there. On the other hand, it would be a long drawn-out process with lots of money asked for. As we drove along, motorbikes with jeering men sped up beside us with another car carrying Mr White Shirt quickly gaining on us. We decided to register.

As we entered the district centre we drove straight up to the only standing concrete building. It was a 1950s-style, brutally angular structure. We later found out that the Belgians had built it just before they left, to prepare the country for independence. It could not have looked more out of place. We asked a bespectacled man for the chief, and to the disgruntlement of the petitioners around us he indicated the building. As we were locking up the car, a very small old man dressed in basketball kit came down the steps and welcomed us. He was the *titulaire*, a mayor-like chief.

As we began to explain who we were and what we were doing the compound was rushed—there is no other word for it—by a crowd of people who all began shouting at the chief, at us and at each other all at the same time. Because no-one was speaking French we could understand little, but words such as *mondele* and Plumpy'Nut were easy to pick out. Besides, the body language was clear enough—they were angry with us. Was this all to do with our aggressive haggling over the price of the boat crossing? Surely not. The chief, who it emerged was sick with high blood pressure, eventually invited us into the building with about ten other people, all of whom turned out to be 'officials' of some sort or another. This included the man in the white shirt who, judging by how the other people were treating him, was important. Perhaps our earlier slight of him was rash.

The meeting began peaceably enough in French with the chief introducing himself and asking us to explain who we were and what we were doing. Chloe, whose French was the clearest and temper the calmest, began explaining our story. As we were doing this some other officials came into the room and presented some of the Plumpy'Nut to the chief. There is no other way to describe their actions than as presenting tribute. She finished her brief statement with a request that everyone else in the room identify themselves. Everyone did except the man in the white shirt. We had an assortment of different officials: the tiny chief, his two towering deputies (both decorous, educated gentlemen), the chief of police in an Adidas track suit, two from the immigration (DGM) department (Lomela is about as far as it is possible to get from the international borders of the DRC), the secret service (the ANR, nicknamed *la N* or *la haine*, meaning 'hate' in French), the army and some other assorted bureaucrats.

By this point we were particularly weary of *la haine*. The agents of the National Intelligence Agency (Agence Nationale de Renseignements, 'a particularly notorious outfit' [Trefon 2011]), are, according to Amnesty International, among the most frequent torturers of the population whom they terrorise. Though their official remit is national security they openly harass the population to extort money and are known to arrest journalists and human rights campaigners, holding them incommunicado in reportedly inhumane conditions. They were by far the worst government agency that we had to deal with, most certainly because they were used to acting with complete impunity.

Ignoring the fact that the man in the white shirt had not introduced himself, we turned to the chief of police, amusingly enough called Captain Martin (I had just left the British Army as a captain and my surname is Martin), and passed on the regards of the colonel in Lodja, his boss. The chief seemed satisfied and Captain Martin announced to the room that we had the permission of the provincial police commander to travel through the district and that we were tourists. Silently we all thanked Carlos for the introduction in Lodja. Captain Martin would be happy to give us advice about crossing the N'djali, he said.

The man in the white shirt clearly disagreed. 'It is impossible that they remain here. There is no letter of permission for them to travel here; they must have a letter of permission,' he finally stated in French. The two individuals in the DGM nodded vigorously to back up Mr White Shirt. We were fairly used to this by this point in the journey and we explained that we had already been to see the minister in Kinshasa and that one no longer needed to have permission to travel through the country. 'Impossible,' he said, talking over Chloe and refusing to look at her. We were getting nowhere.

Chloe, who was establishing herself as the best negotiator as she was able to remain calm in the face extreme provocation, took another tack and suggested that we register ourselves with the DGM as required. Captain Martin emphasised that this would be a good idea. He explained as discreetly as he could to the *titulaire* that he was very busy at the moment because a rape had occurred in the town that day, and in a separate incident one of his officers had been beaten up by a crowd when he tried to make an arrest, but that he would speak to us afterwards when he returned. The normality of such violence was chilling. He left the room.

The DGM officers had by now collected the passports from the chief, who really was looking fed up and ill. As usual they took them outside as there was not enough light inside the old colonial building to examine them properly. I followed to keep an eye on the passports, but also to take myself away from the enraging discussion in the room.

Charlie and Chloe continued debating the issue with the reduced crowd. Finally it transpired that the man in the white shirt was not actually an official at all, but rather the brother of the MP for the area, who in turn was a militia commander from the war. He was the most powerful person in the room, and also our strongest critic. He began accusing us of spying, scoping out where all the minerals were so that we could extract them, and of various other crimes. When we said that one of the reasons that we wanted to travel on our journey through Africa was to improve our French, he scoffed: 'English people who want to speak French, what lies are these?' A case was put together to prove that we were there illegally.

The evidence against us was: a) no travel permit; b) no registration stamps from previous towns (not used in the DRC for at least one year); and c) invalid visas (having confused the date of issue with the date of entry). An Egyptian stamp in my passport sealed the case. Obviously spies. How they thought we'd travelled through so many checkpoints to get to Lomela, the heart of the Congo, remains a mystery. The conversation was bewildering, their suspicion overwhelming. Charlie went to 9Bob to get our maps out and began to show the crowd the route that we had taken since Britain, trying to make some sense of the situation. In retrospect, the more truths we shared, the more incredulous they were, but we were ill equipped to understand this.

Outside I was supervising a fairly energetic rugby scrum over the passports. The DGM officers had control of them, sort of, but there were tens of people who were excluded from the meeting hanging around outside. All of them wanted to hold the passports, and some even appeared to be officials. At the same time a large altercation seemed to be taking place on the road outside the compound involving some twenty people. Suddenly a gunshot rang out from the group. Two seconds later Charlie burst through the door, assuming that he would find me on the floor covered in blood. Instead he found me and the DGM officials laughing at a policeman who, in the middle of the street, had become so frustrated that he had shot his rifle over the crowd. The threshold for violence seemed particularly low in Lomela.

There was nothing to do but laugh, but the situation was anything but stable. Charlie and I stayed on the veranda sharing a cigarette and watching the DGM officers maul our passports. Out of the corner of our eyes, we could see a man with a notebook trying to not look suspicious as he moved towards 9Bob. Barely able to suppress our laughter, we watched him get down on his hands and knees and start sniffing 9Bob, even prodding clods of earth on the tyres and bringing his fingers to his nose. 'What percentage of that is human shit do you think?' asked Charlie drily as we collapsed in laughter. The situation was becoming more surreal by the minute.

At that point Captain Martin came back, now in uniform, and joined the conversation. 'Who is that guy smelling our vehicle?' we asked.

'He is one of my detectives; I told him to come over here and see that you were ok.'

'Do you want to tell him then that we have just driven through 1500 kilometres of human shit and that he will probably catch a disease?'

Captain Martin laughed and we all walked over to the vehicle. Our passports had been returned by now. I went up to the man, who was now actually sniffing the rear left tyre directly, and asked him what he was doing.

'Une investigation, monsieur,' he said pompously, trying to impress his boss. Charlie explained that he was probably going to catch something from 9Bob, and he stood up looking annoyed.

'I need you to explain the military equipment on your vehicle.'

'Of course. What would you like us to explain?'

'This,' he said as he pointed to the collapsible fishermen's chair that we had tied to our roof, 'this is military survey equipment.'

By this point Captain Martin couldn't bear to see his subordinate make a further fool of himself, and dismissed him. We all broke into broad smiles. We had made a friend.

Chloe had meanwhile been talking calmly with the other 'officials' and not getting anywhere. The DGM seemed to have relaxed since taking our details and they were currently away trying to arrange a phone call to their headquarters. We had all hoped to get away—it was only fifteen miles to the crossing. It would be good to get there by nightfall to begin negotiations with the nearest village, which was bound to have an interest in our crossing. When Charlie and I returned to the room the argument was revolving around our security and who would be responsible for it. Chloe repeatedly pointed out that we had just driven nearly 20,000 miles without anyone else being responsible for our security and we would be perfectly fine.

This was becoming infuriating and the position of the man in the white shirt had not changed. He was too superior to talk directly to us, but sat murmuring in the chief's ear: they cannot travel through this area without permission, they must turn back. On reflection, we were the first foreigners to travel through Lomela for a long time and we were proposing to cross a river that hadn't been crossed by a vehicle for fifteen years by building a raft out of oil drums and trees. Looking at it from the outside, it was pretty crazy, though they didn't seemed concerned that we might drown.

The DGM officers then came back from their discussions with Kinshasa. 'It is true, you know,' the slightly older one said, 'they can travel through here with only a tourist visa and their visas are valid.' Mr White Shirt shot them a murderous look, while his friend from *la haine* seemed to snarl. Captain Martin chipped in: 'I will provide security for them, monsieur le chef, while they are in the district. This is what I have been told to do by my colonel.' Mr White Shirt scowled at him and spoke to the chief in a language that we didn't understand. Chloe lost her temper and shouted at him in French that it was extremely rude to talk in a language that not everyone in the room could understand. The chief, whom we were beginning to rather like and feel sorry for, apologetically turned to us in French and asked if we wouldn't mind waiting outside while they had a discussion. Oops.

We went outside and stood around 9Bob in conference-of-war mode. These were by far the most intransigent officials we had met anywhere. Mr White Shirt was something altogether different. Lomela was a highly unstable place and seemed liable to erupt into violence at any time. It was also starting to get late, making it doubtful that we would make the river crossing site before nightfall. We discussed our security and debated whether to break our golden rule of not driving in the dark. Before we had really got underway with this the chief came out dressed in what must have been a Belgian colonial uniform—bright sky blue with a golden sash and raised braided epaulets. He had got changed just to deliver an announcement to us. One of our greatest regrets is that we were not able to photograph this part of the story, but it would not have helped our position to do so.

'We would like you to stay here as our guests this evening. As you can see, there are some problems with your paperwork and we would like to talk to Kinshasa about them. You will be able to go tomorrow morning. We have beds and hot water for you, with a hot meal.'

We looked at each other, all thinking the same things: 'a hot shower...' and 'house arrest in the Congo could be a pretty interesting experience...' We also had very little choice, as we found out shortly after we agreed to stay; even our allies (Captain Martin and the DGM officials) were in agreement: we should stay the night.

As we walked back to the house we could see the chief's wife laying out some chairs and tables for us on the balcony. 'Please, seat yourselves,' said the chief as he went inside to close the meeting with the other officials. Four young policemen were being stationed at the gate—we weren't sure whether they were to stop us leaving or others entering. Either way, Chloe was glad to see them as the looks she had been receiving from the head of *la haine* had been making her feel uncomfortable. As we sat there watching night fall we noticed a tarpaulin covering a car in the corner of the compound. When the chief returned with towels for us we asked him about it.

'It's my car, but there is no diesel here so I cannot use it. It is broken as well.' He went on to explain the whole story—it was actually a donation from the 'foreigners' (an international development agency). Every district chief was meant to have a car so that he could conduct his business but, he said laughing, 'they have clearly never been to Lomela; it broke on the way here from Kinshasa.' Looking at it, we could see that it would never have had the clearance to drive a moderately difficult road. As we knew, the routes were anything but moderate.

We sympathised; he was basically a good man in an impossible position. He went on: 'There is no diesel here, only petrol for the motorbikes, and so I couldn't run it anyway.' The next day we were to find out that the only person with a functioning car in Lomela, apart from us, was Mr White Shirt. We spent an hour or so the following morning trying to fix the chief's car, but there was a Ford-branded part that was needed. In the meantime it was disappearing into the jungle, like everything else in the Congo.

We washed in the bath that the Belgians had left in the house (it also had 'Antwerp' printed on it, like the items in the railway yard). The taps didn't work but we were given half a bucket of hot water each from the kitchen. After that we ate a tasty but small meal of fufu, meat and *feuillage* (cassava leaves) under battery-powered torchlight and went to bed (without mattresses). In many respects the chief did not have many more luxuries than we did on the road, and clearly had had to share his limited food with us. We hoped he and his wife had been able to eat that night. In fact, because we were able to generate electricity with 9Bob we were better off in many ways. It was tragic.

We slept lightly that night. When we got up the chief proudly announced that he had prepared breakfast especially for us. Standing on the table was an old Pernod bottle containing a dark red liquid that he called *jus de berrie*. It tasted like alcoholic earth and was apparently made from tree roots. It was an unbelievably strong firewater and made your chest burn and your temples sweat. Was this how they started their day? We didn't have the heart to insult our host by cooking our usual porridge breakfast, though our stomachs grumbled. Chloe declined more than a sip of the *jus* but Charlie and I dived in, making ourselves dizzy.

Making a show of confidence, I did the morning checks on 9Bob and started warming the engine up and moving the car into a position within the compound where it looked like we were ready to depart. The DGM officials arrived in homemade uniforms and told us that we would have to go back to Kinshasa, that they had made a mistake and they had been wrong the day before. Various other officials trooped in and we convened another meeting in the chief's meeting room, although Mr White Shirt was conspicuous by his absence. We repeated the same points as before, but the officials now focused more on our security than on other arguments. We asked, are we under arrest? We weren't, we were guests, but we still had to go back from where we came. We headed outside for a private discussion.

As we walked out we heard them saying about me in French, 'He is such a hothead, she is sensible, but he is a hothead.' We never really found out what they thought of Charlie, but then he quite likes to be seen as an enigma.

I suggested, and the others agreed, that we would head off slowly to see what would happen, to test their reactions. As we moved the car to the gate of the compound, the only other car in Lomela chose that moment to drive in, completely blocking our path. Mr White Shirt was driving, and sitting next to him was someone in what looked like an official Congolese Army uniform. We sat there staring at each other, each indicating the other to turn back. Both cars inched forward until their bumpers were touching. The others told me off for winding him up.

I switched the engine off, turned to them and said, 'What do you want to do? I think that we need to get the embassy involved; this is ridiculous.' Chloe strongly disagreed—she rather liked the chief and didn't want to cause trouble—but Charlie agreed with me: 'we probably won't even be able to get through, but we should bluff, these guys have no interest in us going forward.' So we got several mobile phones, local and roaming, and a sat phone out, and could not get any of them to work. Shit. While Charlie sat with the phone bluffing and pretending to talk into it, I walked back into the chief's house and addressed the assembled crowd, including Mr White Shirt and the army officer. This was all a bit of a gamble considering how unstable everything was here.

'You say that we are here as guests. We want to leave and you are stopping us. We consider this is an illegal arrest. If you do not let us leave, we are going to call the British embassy in Kinshasa and tell them that we have been arrested illegally by the officials of Lomela.'

There was complete silence in the room. I walked up to the chief, shook his hand and said, 'Thank you very much for your hospitality, monsieur, we will be waiting outside. We are ready to leave now.' When I got back outside, the others still had not had any luck with the telephones. This was a monumental bluff, there was no signal. We couldn't work out what was going on—they clearly wanted us to turn back, but was all this to extract a bribe? It seemed too extreme. What did they not want us to see up ahead? We were still mulling this over when Captain Martin came out and informed us that we could go on condition that we took a police escort. We readily agreed, and even agreed to buy the fuel for his motorbike. After half an hour of arrangements we were off. Mr White Shirt smiled as we left, and the toad from *la haine* smirked and leered at Chloe. It was difficult not to punch him in the face.

Lomela itself was not much of a town. The chief's house and the old post and telecommunications office (long since defunct) were the only concrete structures that we saw. Beyond this, the town itself only seemed to consist of a roundabout with a few shopping shacks and some people sitting around looking bored. There were one or two motorbikes. We got out of 9Bob to buy some dough balls and realised that most of the shacks were one deep from the road and behind them was the jungle. There was nothing here, yet there were more than ten officials in this town because it was a district centre. Captain Martin explained that the officials had responsibility for the whole district, but that it was all jungle and they never had any fuel so were not able to visit any of the villages. It was exceptionally weak governance. We followed his directions to the N'djali river, and to our great delight the start of the road had been pisted.

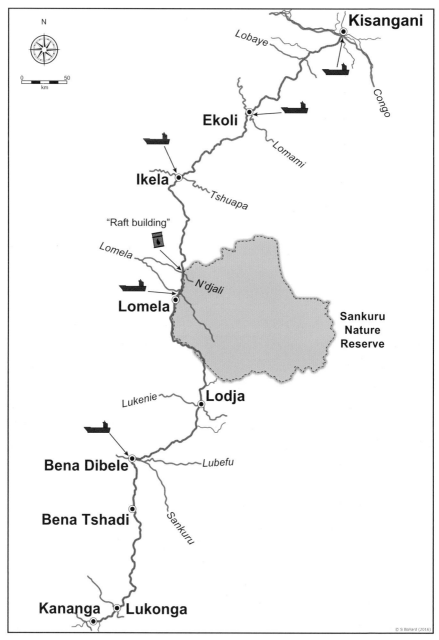

N

0   50
km

Kisangani

Lobaye

Congo

Ekoli

Lomami

Ikela

Tshuapa

"Raft building"

Lomela

N'djali

Lomela

Sankuru
Nature
Reserve

Lukenie

Lodja

Bena Dibele

Lubefu

Bena Tshadi

Sankuru

Kananga   Lukonga

© S Ballard (2016)

Stage 2: Kananga to Kisangani

Chapter 4

Lomela

Day 36: Lomela to just outside Lomela – 5 miles
Day 37: Just outside Lomela to N'djali river – 16 miles
Day 38: Bridge strengthening – 2 miles
Day 39: Raft building

About a mile along the road there was a tree; a big tree, lying on its side across the road.

Wondering what else could go wrong, we began to get the axes and machetes out of the vehicle. We took turns, including the policemen, to chop the tree trunk so that we could move it out of the way and get past. The assembled villagers reported that it had been knocked down by a storm the night before. We looked carefully at the trunk where it had shattered and split. There was no evidence of lightning, and none of us remembered a storm. Wet sap was still oozing out of the splintered trunk: it had clearly been felled very recently. At first we denied that it was possible—surely they hadn't done this just to stop us?

Charlie jogged about 200 yards forward around a bend. There was another tree cut down. And then another. And then another. We questioned Captain Martin about this. 'It was the MP's brother,' he said, stating the obvious. But the only reason he would give was that he thought Mr White Shirt was convinced we were lying and our papers were incorrect. It was an unconvincing answer, and not for the first time we wondered what we were getting ourselves in to. After a quick discussion we decided that as long as Captain Martin was helping us, and friendly, we would carry on. It was only a few trees.

The next few trees were saplings only and we began to get into the swing of it. The machetes were new and very sharp. We worked out that by cutting wedges of trunk out of the felled trees we could usually break them in two by hooking them up to 9Bob and reversing. This would then create a space that we could manoeuvre around. We were relatively cheerful and we entertained lumberjack fantasies. The fifteenth or so tree, however, was of a different scale. The main trunk was thick: at least three feet in diameter. This then split into a 'Y' with the two upper half-trunks about one and a half feet thick. There was enough foliage to completely block the track, and because the tree had been felled at forty-five degrees to the road rather than straight across it would not be a question of simply chopping the trunk. There were several layers to get through, so much so that we looked to see if it would be easier to make a track through the jungle just to the side of the road.

Finally we decided on a plan of action. If we could chop one of the half-trunks through, and clear away as many of the small branches and foliage as possible, it might be possible to set the winch up using another massive tree in the jungle as an anchor and pull what was left of the main trunk just far enough for 9Bob to fit down the other side of the road. We needed to move the main trunk about three feet, and because of the angle between that tree and the anchor it looked like we might just have enough of a turning moment.

The alternative—chopping through the main trunk—was just too much to bear, especially as we were all starting to tire and our soft urban hands were beginning to blister. As we discussed our plan we began to notice that lots of villagers of both sexes and all ages were standing on the banks of the roads staring at us. It was not malevolent, but it was not exactly friendly either. Our attempts to talk to them to find out what was going on were met with silence, and our requests that they help us were met with laughter. We returned to work.

It was not long before the pair of DGM officials, among the most reasonable and nice of those we met in the whole of the Congo, came to visit us. They had changed back out of their uniforms. It was clear that they were being put up to come and see us, and, appealing to Chloe, they suggested that we head back to Lomela to discuss the situation 'for our own safety'. They evaded more specific questions. By now we were all very stubborn and we completely refused, reasoning that they would just put another fifteen trees in our path that we would have to clear to get back to the same place. They threatened us and said that we must go back for our own safety. Pointedly, I asked them if we were under arrest, and they said that we weren't. We replied that in that case we were not interested in returning. If they wanted to officially arrest us, then we of course would go back to Lomela, where we would speak to our embassy. Otherwise they might as well go home because we were busy clearing the trees that Mr White Shirt had ordered to be chopped down! It was desperately sad really; the tree that we were currently hacking to pieces was beautiful and majestic in its size.

As we were finishing our conversation with the DGM guys, Mr White Shirt turned up drunk and began laughing at us. We ignored him, and Captain Martin took him back to Lomela. A junior policeman in a bandana then began harassing the pedestrian traffic for 'une donation, une contribution' by standing in the small gap in the foliage where you could get through and not allowing people to pass without giving him some money or food from their baskets. This was more of a problem, quite apart from the fact that it was wrong (although our moral boundaries were by now blurring). His actions had the potential to turn a neutral crowd into a hostile one, and we tried to get him to stop. It did provide the benefit, however, that most of the villagers departed.

We continued chopping and hacking and after two and a half hours we were beginning to make a dent. By this stage we were getting on very well with our police escort of three or four, and they were even helping us with machete work in places. The blisters on our hands were now starting to bleed and so we bound them in cloth and wore a glove on our chopping hands. As we took more weight off the main trunk of the tree by hacking off limbs, we were able to click the winch another two or three ratchets, which moved the main trunk another couple of inches. As long as the winch held, this would work, but we had several discussions about whether the winch could take it—we were concerned that if it failed, the backlash, with flying ropes and blocks of tackle as well as a falling tree, could seriously damage someone. We didn't have much choice and so continued hacking, slashing and chopping. Every time we clicked the winch, one person did it alone, and the others stood back, trying to keep the assembled onlookers out of the line of fire.

Every so often a group of villagers would walk past and ask us what we were doing. Repeating that we were tourists had almost become a mantra for us. They nodded knowingly—was the word 'tourist' a euphemism for something in the Congo? DRC was the first place that people had asked us if we were 'tourists'—rather than asking which NGO we worked for, or if we were missionaries, as they had done in West Africa.

We could tell by the smiles on their faces that they thought we were lying. Why shouldn't they? Last night they had been told by Mr White Shirt (or someone else) that the road had to be blocked with trees because there were some foreigners claiming to be tourists who needed to be stopped. All attempts by us to work out who they actually thought we were failed. By this point several of the villagers had started on the *jus* and were getting fairly boisterous. We were very glad of our police escort. One man in particular was drunker than the rest and started heckling Chloe in French and asking her what a white woman thought she was doing there and why she was chopping a tree up. He called her a *chinko-blei* (a derogatory term for Belgian in a local dialect) one more time than she could bear. She let loose an indignant torrent of frustration in French and swung round to face the man, forgetting the machete in her hand. It ended up pointing at his face with about three inches to spare. The man was terrified, and Charlie rushed to disarm her, surprised to see her finally lose her temper. She had finally snapped.

'Look we're just tourists, we're just travelling through your country, we have driven from London and never encountered people so inhospitable. You should be ashamed. We don't want to chop this beautiful tree up. These guys,' she said gesticulating at the villagers who were staring open-mouthed, 'these guys cut them down last night to stop us travelling on our journey.'

'What do you mean you are tourists? You are conservationists coming to set up a reserve for the bonobo monkey. Don't lie.'

We all looked at each other, letting his comments sink in. Conservationists? Charlie said, 'He thinks we're conversationalists.' We all cracked up and started laughing. Everyone had a particular group persona that they acted out, and Charlie's was playing the fool. The crowd was staring at us wondering what on earth was going on. Here were three *blancs*, filthy, sweaty, holding axes and machetes, practically rolling on the floor with laughter. We started cracking jokes about the art of making good conversation.

'Ok, so just to be clear. You think we are here to set up a reserve?' Chloe said.

'Aren't you?'

'No. We are on holiday. We hate trees. Who are you?'

'I'm François. I am the tribal chief here. I thought it was a bit weird that you were cutting up the trees. So you are tourists.' (We had also cut down several trees unnecessarily when we thought that it might have been easier to take a route through the jungle.) His last comment was more of a statement than a question.

We looked at Captain Martin for confirmation and he nodded. When I asked him why he hadn't told us he shrugged and looked sheepish. Not wishing to damage a relationship with a key ally, we didn't push it. I asked François who had told all of the locals to cut down the trees on our route. He shook his head. He wasn't going to tell us. We started to talk.

François was a quarter Belgian. His grandfather was a Belgian administrator who had married a local tribal princess. Although he could barely stand through drunkenness he spoke beautiful French, putting our efforts to shame. He was the most educated person we had so far met in the district, and although he had not travelled extensively he had a knowledge of the outside world. His father had held a Belgian passport when alive, but— and we never worked out why—they had not managed to pass the nationality down. He looked slightly wistful as he recounted this particular fact. He was a good man. He spoke about his family and his son. After a while he shook our hands with a smile and staggered off.

We were nearly there with this behemoth of a tree. We started to position 9Bob in place so that we could see how much more was required. Two more clicks on the winch and we were there. Chloe edged him through while

Charlie scouted ahead. He came back just as we were reloading all of the ropes, blocks, axes, machetes, gloves, lever bars etc. back into the car.

'We've got a few more small ones and then there is village about 500 yards up the road,' Charlie briefed us.

It was getting late and we were numbingly exhausted. We asked Captain Martin whether he thought it would be ok if we slept in the village. His response made it clear that he wasn't used to asking permission from the population for anything. When we arrived in the village we asked all the same whether we could stay for the night. The headman replied that it was no problem at all in a manner that suggested that it was a completely normal occurrence for three foreigners to want to sleep there. (And all the while some bizarre game of power chess was occurring between the foreigners and various elements of the local 'authorities'.)

Charlie and Chloe began setting up camp. I walked ahead with Captain Martin to judge the route forward. What I saw… what I saw… made my mouth drop open. Leading out of the village the road followed a gully about ten feet wide with banks about five or six feet deep. The gully had been filled with chopped and felled trees. I climbed over some and managed to go about 100 yards, but it carried on. The whole gully had been completely blocked to the extent that it wouldn't have mattered if we had been clearing a route out of primary jungle—there would have been the same amount of material to remove. Captain Martin laughed when he saw my face and said, 'On va faire demain.'

Returning to the campsite, we wearily prepared for the evening. We prepared our own food: a big bowl of rice and beans flavoured with dry fish. Captain Martin walked over to a group of village women who were watching us curiously, clapped his hands like he was shooing children and demanded that they cook him some food. We didn't like it one bit, but were glad that he was there, so said nothing. He told us that he had been ordered by his colonel to keep us safe and so he, and six armed police, would stay with us. Other than rifles they had no equipment at all, and so we strung out a mosquito net and gave them some bedding to sleep with.

As we sat around our stove cooking and smoking, we managed to get the story out of Captain Martin as to what was going on. It came out in dribs and drabs, as he both did and didn't want to tell us what was going on, and slowly we pieced together the bizarre, twisted world of Lomela. A world of illegal mining, factional disputes, rebel groups and exploitation. Distrust and conspiracy pervaded everything. This is what we understood. It probably represents a fraction of the reality.

Mr White Shirt was from a rebel group that had controlled this part of the country during the civil war. The rebels had worked as a proxy to the government. Their wealth, and his wealth, came from the illegal (although what was legal and illegal in this part of the Congo was a moot point) mining of what everyone there called 'mercure rouge' (red mercury). We never really worked out what 'mercure rouge' was—amusingly (or sadly) we discovered later that it is a hoax substance which conspiracy theorists and occasionally unwitting minor terrorists link to atomic energy among other things. At times, 'it' has traded for fantastic amounts of money, but no-one really knows if 'it' actually exists.

To us, later, the irony that we were being offered a made-up substance in Lomela entirely fitted the parallel universe that we entered during those days. At the time, we assumed that they were talking about coltan, a metallic ore used in making the capacitors found in all electronic devices. The world saw a massive surge in demand for the commodity in the 2000s with the increase in ownership of cell phones, computers and other electronic goods. It is estimated that anywhere between 10 and 60 per cent of the world's coltan reserves can be found in the Congo, and up to 90 per cent of young men in areas such as Lomela have turned from farming to mining as a source of ready money. The implications of the industry in funding militias and the ongoing conflicts are obvious.

The wealth of Mr White Shirt and his family was spread around. But it was mainly spread around Kinshasa to make sure that he was allowed to continue his business unimpeded. That was why the bridge had not been rebuilt since the war: Mr White Shirt's clan/militia did not want any through-traffic in their fiefdom. But, like all petty warlords, they were greedy and didn't look after everyone properly. The local police, for instance, did not feel that they were getting their share so the police colonel and Captain Martin were protecting us. (The police also thought that we were here to exploit the 'mercure rouge' [Tourists? In Lomela?], and they thought that by supporting us they might open up the market). Finally, the titulaire, the sweet old man in the Belgian-style colonial uniform, was completely bought by Mr White Shirt.

Captain Martin continued in a hushed whisper. It was not that any of what he was telling us was not known to everyone else in the district, just that he didn't want people to know that he was telling us. There was a mine very near where we were sitting, in fact, between us and the bridge that was destroyed. So when we had turned up in the district stating that we were heading for the bridge, we were going to build a raft to cross it, and we were tourists from England who were driving across Africa to learn French, Mr White Shirt unsurprisingly assumed that we weren't who we said we were. Much later on in the trip, we actually learnt that the word 'tourist' was a euphemism in Congolese French for someone who came to exploit. This was because this is what all the people who had previously come to exploit the Congo had called themselves. There were no real tourists here.

But what to do with us? Our paperwork was in order. We were threatening to call the British embassy. That was the last thing that Mr White Shirt wanted. We had to be allowed to continue, but we mustn't be allowed to get near the mine. So, in the deepest irony imaginable, the chief was persuaded to issue an order to all the village headmen along the route: we were conservationists who were coming to set up a nature reserve and we wanted to stop the local people from being able to hunt in the forest or chop down trees. We were to be stopped by chopping all the trees down in our path. He said that we were more interested in the trees than the local people.

Lomela operated on its own logic: to the local people a reserve would have been a complete disaster. They lived off what they could hunt and forage for in the jungle. They never quite understood our lives when we explained that we had to buy food at home rather than just finding it, and they certainly couldn't transition to that kind of lifestyle. We had to be stopped. We learnt that this had happened just in front of us and had only begun that morning when we had threatened to call the embassy. They had slowed us with a couple of trees and set to work properly blocking the route further up. In fact, when the drunken Mr White Shirt had turned up earlier when we were tackling the massive tree, he was returning from supervising the destruction further up.

We contemplated this in stunned silence. Even by the standards of the last forty-eight hours it was a lot to digest. Captain Martin told us that he was posting a sentry, and then went to bed. We tried to work out how to interpret the information. We were stuck in a factional war over a made-up substance deep in the Congo, surrounded by a population who thought we were out to take away their livelihoods. The only thing we had protecting us were six policeman who, with the best will in the world, would not do so if push came to shove. I had had a fair amount of experience working with police in Afghanistan, and could see that these guys were just kids with badges. We could hear from their snores that they were already asleep—so much for the sentry.

We had to sleep. We were drifting off on the spot, even though we needed to discuss this latest development. We decided that we would push on, dependent on our police escort, and providing that we felt that local villagers were not becoming too threatening. I suggested that we posted our own sentry that night—at least one of us should be awake at any time sitting in a chair with a machete and the large Maglite torch. We were most vulnerable when we were asleep and the police were not at all to be relied upon. Charlie and Chloe, both utterly exhausted, said that they wouldn't be able to cope tomorrow if they couldn't sleep. It wasn't necessary, they said. The discussion went backwards and forwards, but I insisted. I felt a heavy responsibility for everyone's safety.

We had previously loosely discussed areas of final authority: Chloe's was anything medical or health related (and there were times when she had to insist on certain drug regimes for Charlie and me) and mine was anything to do with safety and security. I put my foot down, volunteered for the worst, middle period (as my sleep was disrupted) and laid down what the duties of the sentry were and what was to be done if certain things happened. This was the only time in a lifetime of travelling in some fairly adventurous places that any of us had slept with a posted sentry. Luckily, the night passed without event.

We were up the next morning early, still picking wood chippings out of our hair. Our tree-chopping muscles ached from unaccustomed use. We had breakfast and did our checks on the vehicle. We sharpened all of the axes and machetes with the metal file from the tool kit. It was going to be a long day. We had planned to start at seven, but Captain Martin was not keen to go. 'I am waiting for orders as to whether we can continue.' This didn't sound good. We bluffed that we would wait half an hour and then would continue anyway, but we didn't think it would be possible to continue without him. When I went over at seven-thirty he was sitting there with another policeman from Lomela whom I didn't recognise. They had a dead monkey with its tail shoved through a hole in the bottom of its jaw, thus making it a convenient carrying handle. It was repulsive.

'Do you want some monkey? I have been ordered to go back to Lomela, but I wanted to cook this. Come and eat with me.'

We weren't sure whether this was a test as to whether we were conservationists or not, but either way we were not eating monkey. We indicated that we were going to continue with or without him. He said that he would order his two policemen to stay with us, but he had to go. None of us liked this very much. He had been a very useful ally, and it felt like we were gradually getting more and more exposed. After a quick discussion we decided to carry on, but with a twist. The villagers had chopped the trees down in the first place and they could help us to clear them as well, although of course we would pay. This might also have the added benefit of bringing the villagers onside once they saw that they could earn money from us. Chloe gave the headman our offer, and asked him to spread the word. No-one came forward. This was going to be a long day.

We soon got into the swing of it. Most of the trees in the gully were small to medium sized. This meant that with a few carefully placed hacks we could snap and drag the tree limbs out of the way using 9Bob and the tow ropes. We told the two policemen that we would pay them a dollar if they began chopping and worked for the day. They enthusiastically agreed, shouldering their AK47s and attacking the foliage with relish. Crowds of villagers stood on the banks of the road watching us, talking quietly and generally looking fairly sullen. Occasionally we would fall into conversation with one of them, and we would use the opportunity to try to dissuade them of the idea that we were conservationists. 'We don't care about the trees, look at how we are chopping them.'

There was one particular man to whom we spoke at some length, and we could see that the mood was starting to change. He was a trader. He grew his tomatoes and other produce, and took them into the district centre strapped to his bike. He couldn't get to market today because the road was blocked. He hadn't heard any of the back story, so we told him about Mr White Shirt and the villagers chopping the trees down to stop us.

'This is disgusting,' he said. 'Again, again, again, our leaders are lying to us. And using us. And blocking the roads and destroying the trees and the forest. It is too much,' he said with some emotion. We empathised and said we were sorry for causing all the trouble, but we were just trying to travel through. If the villagers could help us clear the road, and we would pay them, then we would be gone much quicker. We repeated the offer to the villagers. 'A dollar, a meal at midday, and all the water and cigarettes that you need.' People began to talk amongst themselves. 'A dollar!'

While this was occurring we had taken our eyes off the policemen who were 'protecting' us. We suddenly noticed one was missing. The other looked slightly sheepish and said that he had just popped back to Lomela. He offered to go looking for him, and disappeared never to return. We had just lost our police protection. It didn't take long to realise that he had stolen a machete—value $8—rather than carry on working—wage $1. This was a huge blow. We only had one of these broad, wedge-shaped machetes left and they were proving to be the best tools that we had for getting through the wood. But the policeman had, unwittingly, given us more than he had taken. As soon as the crowd realised what had happened, it erupted. 'They are always stealing from us as well. They are such thieves'.

We repeated our offer and got the merchant to repeat it to the crowd in a local language. We think he also explained that we were just travellers and the chief had lied to them when he told them that we were conservationists. People started to come forward and offer themselves for work. What we had been so scared of—losing our police escort—had actually turned out to be a blessing and we began to wonder how much of the previous hostility that had been directed towards us was because we had been with the police. We quickly bad mouthed the police so as to reposition ourselves under the protection of the people, trading one set of allies for another. We were learning very fast that we had to be fickle. We had more workers volunteering than we could use, and so we selected three of the strongest looking.

From then on our progress became steadier. One of us permanently manned the vehicle, which we used to provide dragging power and also to store any tools, ropes etc. when they weren't in use—we couldn't afford to lose any more equipment as there would be no way to replace it before Kisangani, which was about 250 miles away. The second person worked at the coalface, so to speak, directing the work crew as to what to cut in which order so that we could then drag it out of the way. This individual also received instruction from the workers on machete and axe technique. The third person would either be scouting ahead, cutting or talking to the crowd. This last role was important because we were completely alone and needed to maintain our coalition, gather information and spread the message that we were not a threat. We began to ask about the route to the bridge. We had to make a particular turning, they said: we definitely had to go one way, and not another way. It was very important, they said. We understood that the other route led to the mine, which was, we now heard, managed by two Belgians. The plot thickened.

We made good ground with our crew. Some of them decided that they didn't really like working and so slunk off, but there were plenty of other volunteers willing to take their place. We stopped for lunch and stood around the bonnet of 9Bob where Chloe had cooked a big pot of beans and rice for the workers and us. We all ate out of the same bowl and drank out of the same bottles. We had to build this team, and by doing little things like this were sending signals that it was good to be on our side and part of our crew.

The workers puffed out their chests with pride and showed off to the other villagers how great the *mondeles'* food was. For the first time in a couple of days we felt like we might get through.

After lunch we settled into a rhythm of chopping and dragging. In places the trunks, branches and foliage came to one and a half times the height of us. We found ourselves swinging axes above our heads. We learnt how unsuited we were to this type of work, although Charlie was at least built physically for it. The heads of our axes kept unpredictably and dangerously slipping off and one or two of the work crew who were lumberjacks went to fetch their own superior tools. The speed with which they were able to go through a tree really showed how weak and unskilled we were. We started to take a more 'efficient' supervisory role, enjoying being serenaded by a young man with a small three-string guitar carved out of a single piece of wood, and a troop of boys too young to chop for long, who took to dancing on the obstacles instead. The advantage of the large crowd was that they could now accurately explain the situation to the irate *velo* men trying to push their loads through the foliage.

Finally, we came to the tree of trees.

It must have been ancient—and taken a while to fell in the first place. It made our hearts ache to see the waste, as well as making us worried the game was up. Lying at ninety degrees to the route, forking into two equally massive trunks, it was so big that we would have had to chop it in several pieces to drag it out of the way with 9Bob if we even had tow straps long enough to tie around it. It would take forever and might not be technically possible, even with the crew. Watching the workmen walk up the outstretched branches to take a seat on the giant trunk, Chloe casually pointed out that we could use the trees and branches that we had already chopped to create a ramp (of around six feet) to drive over the two great trunks of this tree. It was so audacious a plan that it might actually work. The whole thing was like a massive obstacle course over which we had to get a two-ton Land Rover.

While this was being planned and prepared I went and scouted ahead. There were only another 100 yards or so to go. Heavily blocked, but nothing that we

couldn't handle. After that, it appeared to open out and there were no more blocked roads. I also spoke to an old man leaning against a tree and drunk on palm wine, who confirmed that there were no more felled trees in-between us and the bridge. I also made sure he got the message that we weren't a threat and we were just passing through. He smiled and nodded: he had already heard. I came back with the good news just as the finishing touches were being put to the ramp.

Even by our standards it was a bold move. Two on-ramps had been built out of bundles of branches about the girth of one's arm. These led up to the first massive trunk. Between the two trunks, the team had placed the waffle boards, and then leading off there were two similarly constructed off-ramps, bound together with creepers. Charlie and Chloe lined the vehicle up but could not get 9Bob to climb onto the steep on-ramp so we moved the waffle boards to create an on-ramp to the on-ramp. This we were able to get 9Bob to mount, and once his front wheels were balanced on the first huge trunk, I moved the waffle boards to bridge the gap between the two trunks while Chloe held 9Bob on the clutch. This bit was absolutely critical as if 9Bob fell between the two trunks it would take days to get him out. You could feel the crowd holding their breath above the noise of the engine.

Chloe edged the vehicle forward and luckily the wheels 'bit' onto the waffle boards rather than just pushing them forward into the gap. Slightly more forward and the front wheels were on the off-ramp. At this point the waffle boards needed repositioning as the back wheels would have missed them completely. Once that was done and the back wheels had mounted them successfully it was all downhill—as the full weight of 9Bob fell onto the off-ramp, it started snapping, but Chloe gunned the engine and took 9Bob off. The cheer from the crowd was deafening—they were getting more into it than we were. With our exhaustion, and as a result of the pressure we were under, we could only manage weak smiles.

Our thoughts then turned to the next problem while we cleared the last of the felled trees. Clearly someone very powerful (at least in the local area) had invested significant effort in stopping us from going where we wanted to go. We were concerned that this person might try to kidnap us or worse. We didn't think it was very likely, but it would be very easy to make us disappear, and we had to consider all the possibilities and eventualities and try to plan for them. We felt we had done reasonably well at getting the local villagers onside, but we didn't know whether Mr White Shirt—or someone else—would make a last ditch effort.

We decided that we would push on (we could hardly turn back) until the moment when we had weapons pointed at us (assuming we had that much warning). Then we would capitulate immediately. We ran through a few scenarios of how this might happen, a roadblock manned by a militia for example, and how we would deal with it. We had been carrying a small satellite tracker since the UK, and we sent a signal with our location. This then sent an email to Chloe's dad. We also all refreshed ourselves on how to use the panic setting on the device (which would send a different message to Chloe's dad) and discussed how one of us would attempt to send a signal while the other two distracted our kidnappers. We didn't believe that this was a probability, but after the last three days we didn't know what to expect anymore.

By this time we had cleared the last of the gully and once again we were facing the open road. We were in the situation that we had been in three days ago: only fifteen miles to get to the bridge! First, we had a crowd of workers to pay. The money was hidden in various places around the car and so once we had got everyone around one side of the car we got some out of one of the hiding places. There was now quite a crowd milling around so I got inside the car and doled the money out through a half-opened window. Each man would come up and we would quickly discuss how many hours he had done. We would then explain to the worker what we were paying him and why. We did this for the whole line, and in one case brought one of the workers back and paid him a tiny bit more to make it as fair as we possibly could across the group. For most of them, it was their first ever pay day, and it was very civilly completed. There were no arguments and no snatching of money. We were again grateful to Alfred who had told us previously what the day rates for labourers were in the area.

Once we had finished this, many of the workers asked if they could come with us. They saw the prospect of more work, yes, but they also saw the prospect of something new, some adventure, some experiences. Most of them had never left their villages. It was a poignant moment. We explained that we didn't know if we would need them and that we were travelling a long way. Between ourselves we knew that we would be able to find workers wherever we were. The Congo was not short of people. Anyway, employing workers wherever we were was a good way of developing local relations, which we would not enjoy if we imported our own workers with us.

After a long discussion we drove off, and some of our former workers climbed onto the back of the car or hung on rather pathetically. Our hearts broke—they just wanted to get out of their lives—but for us this was a problem as the roof rack and other fixtures would not take that kind of weight—9Bob was already doing far more than he should have been asked to do. In the end we had to drive off with Charlie and me hanging off the car literally beating the guys away. It was a sad end to a happy relationship.

Not really having time to digest this experience, as we thought that we were about to be ambushed by armed men at any moment, we ran through our contingency plans. We passed through empty villages on fairly good roads until up ahead we could see the landmark that we had been told about—the bifurcation. We slowed slightly and scrutinised the tree lines looking for possible ambush sites or faces in the trees. No-one. As we reached the fork, we saw the tribal leader, François, from a couple of days ago, sitting with two other men, just waiting. He stared at us. We stared at him. We turned towards the bridge, and away from the mine. A few hundred yards later on he sped past us on a motorbike heading in the same direction. We didn't really know what was going on but, as with during the rest of the trip, there was nothing to do except keep going. We only had three miles until we got to the bridge and it was starting to get dark.

About a mile short of the crossing point we passed through a village with a very basic health clinic. Making a mental note of where we might recruit workers, we continued. The run-up to the river was covered in dense bushes of fifty-foot high bamboo, with more jungle behind. As we descended to the river, the road widened slightly and just before the bridge an embankment had been built up. We had arrived. We were exhausted, especially Charlie, who had been up since three that morning. The adrenaline that had kept us going all day suddenly disappeared, and we could hardly move our limbs. We got down from the car and walked forward to the still-intact bridge over the first river channel or swamp. The bridge was made entirely of bamboo, and there was no way that it would support 9Bob. Once across, we were on an island, which had been slightly built up into a causeway to give the run-up to a second bridge. This one was entirely absent apart from a few charred posts sticking out of the water. Running down from the causeway on the right-hand

side there was a beach—hopefully where we would build and launch our raft. But for now we needed to wash, cook and sleep.

When we got back to the car, we found a delegation from the village led by François. Judging by how they deferred to him, he carried some weight around here, and thankfully he greeted us warmly. We explained that we were completely exhausted and that we needed to sleep but that we would have work for five strong men in the morning. We arranged that they would come at nine with tools. We would be up well before that, but we wanted to plan. We also explained there would probably be three or so days' work, as we had some fairly serious engineering works to carry out. François kindly asked if we needed anything else, and we requested that the women in the village sell us some *feuillage* (the closest approximation to spinach eaten in the jungle). Once they had gone, we collected wood for a fire and put on the same old bean stew. While that was cooking we went to the river and washed ourselves. We went back to the car and ate slowly, eyes drooping as we chewed.

The next morning we were awoken by a massive crowd of people at about seven. François wasn't there, and only a couple of them had rudimentary French. We asked them to wait by the side of the bridge while we got up. Unfortunately a dew had fallen the night before and so our kit was wet and we couldn't put it away immediately. We were entering a part of the river basin that was in its wet season. We made some coffee and stood around debating how to get across the weak-looking bridge.

We could go around it and remake a lower bridge that crossed the swamp it was resting in, or we could look at some way of actually reinforcing the superstructure. The problem was that if 9Bob went into the swamp that would be the end of everything. None of us knew the slightest thing about the structural mechanics of how bridges distributed weight. I wasn't even willing to bluff, which I would willingly do about most things. In the end we settled for laying another bridge on top of the old bridge, in effect as if it wasn't there. We didn't need a whole bridge either, just two tracks wide enough for 9Bob's wheels. So we needed four, very long, very straight tree trunks.

By now François had arrived and we explained what we wanted to do. We had also decided to do everything through him rather than hire the workers individually as we had before. As long as he was cooperative that would work fine and it seemed that everyone wanted us over the river—anything to get us further away from the mine. Later on François told us that the district chief had ordered him to help us in any way possible to get us over the river and out of the district.

François selected a team of five muscular men. Through him we explained to the crew what was required. One of us stayed with the gear, while the other two spread out with the team looking for likely candidates for our needs. In a few instances they began felling trees that were unsuitable despite us asking them not to start until we had agreed the suitability of each tree. But mostly they didn't care about chopping trees down—the forest was full of them, they argued. We began ranging further and further as it became clear that what we were looking for was actually fairly rare. Tree trunks, it turns out, don't grow straight most of the time. Who knew?

One of the workers indicated that we follow him and he led us right back to the village, where there was a grove of palm trees—tall and straight. Perfect. As we stood around debating which exact specimens to fell, we all felt sharp stabbing pains in our ankles. Looking down, we could see mean-looking ants, about the size of a grown man's thumbnail, clamping down on our skin. Charlie tried to pull one off and the body came away in his hands, with the jaw still digging into his skin. Incredibly, our lower legs started to go numb. What was this?

We dashed back to the road and I pulled out a lighter, slowly burning them off one by one as our Congolese team laughed. It was a kindly laugh, unlike the mean taunting that we had experienced before. They were much harder than us. Gradually the feeling in our legs returned and we started laughing as well. Over the next two weeks these ants, aggressively territorial, were to become a feature of the terrain, and we learnt to recognise which particular species of plant they were associated with. Worse were the so-called fire ants. We never actually saw them, but whenever any of us made the mistake of stringing a tow strap or hammock string to a banana tree (usually despite vociferous warnings from watching villagers) we would get a burning pain and the feeling we'd rubbed chilli into a deep cut. This would be followed by numbness and swelling, taking a day to go down. We became skilled at rubbing repellent into our hammock strings at night to stop insects climbing on us and biting us through the hammock silk.

And then, one day, we never met them again. Such was the biological diversity of the Congo. Animals and insects would appear for a few hundred miles and then disappear again. We half joked that the vast majority of them were unknown to modern science, although they were very familiar to our Congolese friends. For one, thankfully short, period we passed through the land of brightly coloured (and one assumes poisonous) spiders. We would be driving along and a luminous turquoise, red and yellow, or lime-green specimen would fall through the window onto someone's knee; we would then have to very gently encourage it to head back to the forest.

The guys began felling the trees. Once the first one was felled we again ventured into the forest, with our trousers tucked into our socks like geeky maths teachers cycling to school. The trunk was unbelievably heavy, and it was all that seven of us could do, heaving with all our strength, to get it onto the road. There was no way we were going to be able to drag it the mile or so back to the bridge site. Charlie stayed to supervise the remaining felling and I went back to get 9Bob. Returning to the palm grove, we used the tow ropes to drag the trunks behind the car. Even then it required using the low range gearbox to get 9Bob moving. All of this effort took some time, and it was after midday by the time that we got all four trunks down to the bridge site.

In the meantime Chloe had been working on 9Bob and our kit. All of our equipment was in a sorry state after the last few days. She had repacked and cleaned and re-sharpened and oiled. She had also done some maintenance work on the vehicle and got the village women to rustle up some lunch for us and the workers (lunch was part of their day's payment). She did all of this while being in the middle of what can only be described as a circus atmosphere by the bridge. Tens of people were coming and going to see what the mad *mondele* were up to. We were also along the route of an inquisitive stream of *velo* boys. Chloe noticed a number of the women standing around watching were sharing a fruit they called *habam*, with which we were completely unfamiliar.

Excited to see fresh fruit of any kind, Chloe had asked to try some, and the village ladies, laughing, gave her one to split open. We subsequently found out that the fruit is called *Chrysophyllum lacourtianum* and is not found elsewhere. It looks like a pomegranate on the outside, and when split reveals a pink and yellow striped flesh and jackfruit-like seeds. It is sweet and sour at once to taste, and oozes a white liquid which rapidly becomes a gum on contact with the fingers, lips or teeth. Perhaps this is why the women were laughing—Chloe looked like a kid in a sweet shop by the time we returned, unable to get the sticky gloop off her fingers.

It was around now that someone took Charlie to one side and showed him the contents of a cardboard box filled with reddish-brown ore of some sort (although all the soil was that colour too, so it might have just been mud). This was the 'mercure rouge' we'd been told about. He claimed to be able to produce tons of the stuff from a site that he knew in the jungle. Over the next couple of days several others would secretly take one of us aside and show us a small red rock, speaking in hushed tones.

After lunch we started to look at dragging the logs into position over the bridge—a big task. It was clear that we needed more workers. At that moment our workers from the morning also declared that they couldn't work any further unless they had some of the earthy alcoholic drink—some *jus*. We looked at François disbelievingly, but he shook his head, smiled wryly and said, 'C'est le Congo, monsieur.' As a joke, we said to François that we would pay the extra workers we needed in *jus*, an offer which he readily accepted. This was actually a stroke of luck because all day extra workers had been working in the expectation that they would be paid as well.

We had repeatedly explained to François that we could only afford to pay the five workers we had agreed (we were running short of money and still had hundreds of miles to cover before Kisangani). But the booze was so cheap, with the amount they drank equivalent to a few pennies. We couldn't work out why they seemed to accept it in lieu of much bigger cash payments but we didn't push the point. Booze was a way of making our money go further with the only problem being that our crew became drunker and drunker, and more and more unruly, as the afternoon wore on.

Chloe and I hooked up a series of ropes around the first log with handles for multiple men to hold onto in their dragging. They took position and took the strain.

'*Brima!*' shouted the man at the head of the trunk, the word half tumbling out of his mouth in a snatched staccato.

'*Brima!*' echoed the team.

'*Brima!* shouted the leader, and the question-and-answer chanting continued until he was satisfied that they were responding with enough élan. One final time, he shouted '*Brima!*' and they responded '*Hooooooo!*' in deep, strong voices, perfectly in harmony. As they did so they dragged the log a couple of feet, and the sound trailed off as their movement slowed. Charlie

stopped helping, got his camera out and started documenting the scene as they worked to a melody. It was invigorating. We all joined in ... *'Brima!'* ... *'Hoooooooo!'*

We worked to get all the logs into place. Before we could get each end of the log resting onto the bank on either side there was a period when the bridge was taking all the weight of the log and some of the crew heaving it. The bridge swayed and creaked. We got François to issue an order that only essential people were to be on the bridge while this was happening. This meant us and our drunken crew. We were worried that if the bridge collapsed we would have people impaled in the swamp on the broken slivers of sharp bamboo. It was the stuff of nightmares. Our med kit definitely wouldn't be able to deal with a mass casualty event.

Once all the logs were in place, we lashed four trunks together in two pairs. This made a platform on which 9Bob's wheels could balance without slipping down between the two trunks. As we were doing this further crowds of people began to arrive to view the spectacle. Charlie worked with François

to get them all standing in one place away from the bridge while Chloe and I discussed tactics and hand signals. We introduced a new hand signal meaning 'the bridge is collapsing, accelerate as fast as you can to try and get to the other side'. Chloe got in the driving seat and Charlie hushed the crowd. It was incredibly brave of Chloe: had the bridge collapsed, it was hard to see how she would have escaped.

It took several goes to line 9Bob up. I leant the waffle boards against the ends of the trunks creating an on-ramp and 9Bob mounted the logs. Later we would joke that it was like doing gymnastics with a two-ton medicine ball. Chloe moved 9Bob forward slowly and came across the bridge as it creaked. Once or twice we had to reverse 9Bob slightly to realign him so that we could continue going forward. As we got about two-thirds of the way across the crowd started cheering and shouting. Charlie shouted to silence them so that we could all listen to the bridge, which by this stage was swaying slightly.

Chloe came further forward and by now her wheels were over the other bank. Another three feet and they were on the ground. Another and 9Bob was clear. The crowd erupted. To them this was all new, but when Chloe stepped down from the vehicle, white as a sheet, you could see the strain on her face. We limply hugged. It was the first time that we had had any physical contact since breaking up. The villagers queued to shake her hand, each offering excited congratulations.

It had taken all day to get across the river with our crew of, by now, legless workers. We gathered around the vehicle and counted out the money to pay them. Many more than the five we had agreed came forward to claim wages, so we gave the total payroll to François and explained that there was only money for five workers and that we were running out of money. François looked disappointed, but understood. He had had enough experience to see from our faces that we were sincere, and he understood when we explained that we had had to hire workers for the last few days, which was draining our cash. He then went and divided up the money between the workers in some way that he thought fair. We arranged to meet again the next morning.

During our wash that evening, Charlie, a former swimming champion, set out across the river to judge the currents more accurately. I tried to join him, but the flow in the centre was so fast that, although I was also a confident swimmer, Charlie nearly had to rescue me. Once we had washed we made a small fire on the island. Surrounded by tall bunches of bamboo with the river running beside us, we looked up at the stars, talking about the best way to make a raft. It had been about fifteen years since any of us had made one, and then it was only to carry one or two people across a still lake. Necessity spurred us to think hard about the problem—if 9Bob sank, it would be a long walk out.

We had a great night's sleep and the next morning were able to get up early. A small crowd had already gathered, but they were sitting quietly to one side waiting for us. Next to them sat a fresh-faced young man in the smartest variation of DGM uniform we'd seen. Luckily, he was too shy to talk to us. We waved and started our morning routine. Once done, we sat with coffee and cigarettes around a patch of sandy ground and drew in the dust what we thought the raft should look like.

We had the six oil drums which we had tested for buoyancy the previous day. They seemed quite buoyant. How that would translate into floating a two-ton Land Rover (including kit) we were not sure. We could also get as much material as we liked from the forest and we knew that logs floated—but how much? There was also the added complication of the engine. When 9Bob was emptied (we planned to take the stuff over in a separate run) the weight of the engine would make the raft very front heavy. It was all quite fun and the crowd watched in fascination.

After about twenty minutes François turned up and we presented our plan. Each of 9Bob's four wheels would end up with an oil drum underneath it. The drum would be held in place by a framework of trunks and lateral spars. The whole design would be set around three long trunks that ran front to back. This would enable us to put the load-bearing part of the raft at one end of the trunks—and this would hopefully counteract the imbalance created by the weight of the engine. Beyond that, we put the last two drums on either side of the raft lashed as outriggers to create some lateral stability. We were rather proud. François looked at it and only made one comment.

'You cannot use these palm trunks [he meant the ones from yesterday]. Palm is too heavy. You want *tshumbe*. That is what they make the pirogues out of, it is light and it floats.'

As he finished speaking he turned to someone in the crowd and said something in an unknown language. The man got up with his machete and disappeared into the forest. We began to hear some chopping and then he returned with a tree the girth of an arm. We examined the wood and tested its buoyancy—it was very light, just like balsa wood. Perfect. François had already selected the workers—a different five to spread the income in the community—and so we split into teams heading into the forest to look for *tshumbe*, recognising it by its distinct leaves. They were reasonably common but not often straight, which we needed for the raft.

Charlie called out that he had found a specimen and so we all went to have a look. It was tall and straight, and we could probably reuse some of the branches that we cut off it as spars. Wherever possible we had been trying to be economical in our use of trees and only cut down the minimum necessary. In most cases we had to restrain our team from cutting down everything in sight. To them the jungle was an unlimited resource. To be fair to them, it probably would remain as such until commercial logging was set up in the Congo. The workers that day had brought their own tools and we had a very skilled axeman (an axe in Congolese French is a *shoka*). The speed with which he went through massive trunks, even though it was light *tshumbe* and he had had a lot of practice, was impressive. We stood back and admired his work. Unfortunately when the tree fell it took out a further three trees. The Congolese shrugged.

We dragged the tree out to the beach where the raft was going to be constructed. Our plan was to do it half-in/half-out of the water, and I got on with laying out the raft pattern and beginning to lash it together. Thanks to a lot of time in the Boy Scouts and some more time sailing, I knew a few lashings and knots, which I taught the others. A raft only requires a clove hitch and a square lashing, thankfully, and these are simple knots. Charlie and Chloe went back into the forest to supervise the felling of more trees, while I pulled the raft together with some workers. François looked on, offering useful comments or helping me communicate with the crew who didn't speak any French.

By lunchtime we had enough trees felled to make the basic framework. We had also completely run out of rope—despite having bought all of the rope in Lodja. François called a bunch of children together and sent them into the forest to find and collect vines and creepers. We were slightly dubious at first, but they were just as strong as rope. We moved the raft more fully into the water and tried to get the oil drums under the framework in the places that we wanted them, where they would sit under 9Bob's wheels. It proved impossible—the drums were just too buoyant to be forced under the raft.

As we sat aboard the wooden structure, trying to bounce the air-filled drums into place, the men suddenly started calling to one another and pointing to the tree-covered water edge some ten feet away. Chloe looked to François to translate their conversation into French. He told her there was an animal, no two animals, in the water. 'Oh,' said Chloe, 'what kind of animal?' François didn't know the name of the animal in French, but once Chloe had established that it wasn't a crocodile or hippopotamus, she edged closer for a better look. Looping slowly in and out of the trailing limbs of the bankside trees she could see that two otters were playing. 'Oh,' said Chloe, 'they're very rare in our country, protected.' François looked at her excitedly: 'do you know how to catch them?'

We broke for lunch.

As we were eating, more and more people began to gather on both banks of the river. *Mondele* in the river were unusual entertainment, and the *velo* men using pirogues to take their bikes across the river had had plenty of time to spread the word. People had big smiles on their faces, laughing in the carnival atmosphere. Just as we were finishing our meal, our old friend Captain Martin showed up with a big grin.
'Thanks for coming; we could have done with your help earlier.'

'I just wanted to make sure that you were actually leaving the district,' he said, not unkindly, but very truthfully. He then ordered that a table and chair

be brought to him with a bottle of *jus*. He sat himself down comfortably to watch the proceedings. We helped ourselves to his drink. After working in the river water all day we were cold, and the alcohol was welcome. The firewater brought some colour back to our cheeks.

Once we had cleared away lunch we sent the crew out into the bamboo groves to cut as much bamboo as they could. We wanted to use it as a decking for the raft so that 9Bob would be able to (quickly) drive on and off and so we would be able to move about on the raft once it was underway. They were experienced in building from bamboo, and taught us the different properties of old and new poles. As they cut, collected and sorted, we managed to get the oil drums in the right places under the raft and lash them into place. It was starting to take shape and we had great fun jumping up and down on it to see how it floated. When the guys had assembled a reasonable pile of bamboo we fully floated the raft and then began lashing the decking down. It now actually began to look like it might work. By this time Captain Martin was drunk and slurring his words, shouting encouragement to all and sundry while sitting at a school desk and chair on the sandy beach. François chuckled to himself and grinned at me. 'Le Chef,' he said mockingly, nodding to the captain.

It was time now to do the test runs. The plan for crossing was to send across a small group of local guys along with Chloe by pirogue with one end of a couple of the ropes. The other ends would be tied to the raft in places that facilitated some steering if one rope was pulled rather than the other. For the first run I stood alone on the raft. It took about fifty seconds, and if my feet hadn't been wet from before they wouldn't have been wet from that crossing. I ran from side to side. The raft sat high in the water and was stable. The pirogue crew crossed again and pulled me back. The second crossing was slightly more difficult to organise.

We had worked out that an empty 9Bob weighed the same as about thirty villagers (working on about 50kg per villager, which was an underestimate; we counted two 'children' as one 'villager'). There were easily enough people around, but not everyone was keen. François acted as a good role model and understood the need. He stood on the raft and encouraged everyone to get on. We slightly encouraged the festival atmosphere at this point and it worked. We even tried to get Captain Martin on the raft, but he made some excuse about not being allowed legally in the next district (which started in the middle of the river). But he did 'encourage' lots of villagers to get on. We sent the pirogues across again.

This time the raft was much more heavily laden, but the bamboo decking was just out of the water. François and I had the villagers moving from one side to the other to test the stability of the raft. Halfway across one of the children told me with a cheerful grin that he couldn't swim. I grinned back and wondered how many of the other villagers couldn't swim. Thankfully the raft was stable and floated well. Everyone made the return journey safely.

Once everyone was off the raft François came up to us. 'Great, now we can get you across this evening,' he said, hoping to get shot of us as soon as possible. We remembered that the district chief had told him to stay with us until we left the district and were no longer his problem. He also seemed worried that a storm was on its way. We really wanted to help François and to cross before the rain, but it was getting late and it would take some time to shuttle both our kit and 9Bob across. The real worry was that if anything went wrong, we would have precious little time to sort it out before it became pitch black. Captain Martin was under the same pressures from his hierarchy and he was also pushing us hard to make the journey that night.

In the end, we decided it would be foolhardy and that there was too much to lose. We apologised to François and settled in for another night. Before he left, Captain Martin took us to one side and said that he was able to get us tons of coltan if only we could hook him up to a buyer in the West. 'We can go into business together!' It was sad in that it came across as a genuine belief that white people are only interested in the resources of the country and sad, too, that many in the Congo are willing to facilitate the process through their own greed, or need. We made non-committal noises and thanked him for his help.

The next morning we got up before first light and began organising our kit and moving it down to the raft. Next we rolled the empty 9Bob down the near-vertical bank onto the beach. By the time people started arriving we had already half loaded the raft. We had to be quite careful at all times. There were small crowds of people milling about, all looking at our kit. We had to always have one person on the vehicle, another on the raft and the third moving between the two. François helped us with crowd control. We had stripped everything out of 9Bob: the spare tyres, the fuel, the water. It was the first time that we had had everything out since packing him in England and

we found all sorts of things that we had completely forgotten about, as well as a lot of Saharan sand. We were able to move it all across without incident and unloaded it into a pile on the other side with a tarpaulin over it. Leaving Charlie to guard the pile from the less familiar crowd that was gathering in the new district, we returned.

We tied the raft tight to the bank to stop it drifting out when 9Bob tried to drive on. The waffle boards were set up as an on-ramp. The boards and the tow ropes, among the simplest equipment that we had, were to prove utterly essential time and again. As per usual, Chloe drove and I did the hand signals. François stood on the raft ready to shout orders as necessary to various teams of workers: those casting us off, those pulling us in, those receiving us on the other side. There were probably about twenty people involved in the operation.

9Bob easily mounted the waffle boards, but as soon as he got onto the bamboo it splintered and the wheel fell straight through. Reverse and try to repair the raft, or keep going forward? Forward! Now that 9Bob was empty the engine's power was really palpable. Chloe kept edging him forward until each of his wheels sat on top of an oil drum. While the workers cut free the raft and the waffle boards, François and I pushed and heaved to get the raft fully afloat because 9Bob's weight had beached it slightly on the shore. Once that was done, we jumped on the raft and shouted 'Brima!' to the pulling crew on the other shore. Chloe kept the engine running and in gear, and we slowly started to traverse the river. 'Brima!'

'Hoooooooo!'

The raft was partially submerged and 9Bob's wheels were touching water, but it was stable. We were going to make it across. A week of build-up; a minute of crossing.

As we nudged into the other bank I jumped into the water and turned the raft around, while one of the workers started shortening the tree trunks on that end of the raft so that it could get closer into the shore (this shore was steeper than the first one). Chloe reversed 9Bob off without incident. François shook everyone's hand furiously—he seemed to be happier than we were. The only negative in the whole situation was that Charlie had had to sit guard on all of our stuff, which excluded him from the action, but there was no way that Chloe and I could have concentrated on the crossing without the peace of mind that he generated by watching over everything. The other annoying thing was that he had set up a video camera to record the whole event, but it had failed to record, instead deciding to switch itself off.

This episode of the trip always forms a central part of our memories of the two months, partly because it took place in the middle of the trip and in the middle of the Congo. But it had also entailed the most extreme concentration of events and people conspiring both to stop us and help us achieve our goal. Each of these things—the officials, the route blockage, the bridge or the raft—could have spelt a retreat back the way we had come, but somehow, often through luck (if we hadn't met Alfred or François, for instance), we managed to scrape through. In retrospect also, this crossing marked a point of no return—we were more committed than ever now to our journey north. By this stage of the trip we were a very well-oiled machine. Everyone knew what they were doing in their roles, and our relationship issues were quietly unspoken since the challenges required complete concentration and the contribution of the whole team.

With the crossing completed, we set about dismantling the raft. Some people had asked us to keep it in place—we think they saw a taxable asset as no-one had been able to cross that river for twenty years—but we had no idea what to expect over the remaining crossing points before Kisangani. Others begged us to remove it so as to keep Lomela cut off. The N'djali was not even on our list of five crossings, and it had taken us several days to traverse. We were all starting to run out of visa days: Chloe and Charlie both had work starting in London in a few weeks' time. I was also completely broke and had no job to go back to. Previously the plan had been that Chloe would support me while I was job hunting, but this was now obviously off the cards. An element of time pressure had entered the back of our minds.

Once we had dismantled the raft, we watched as bits of it were picked up by the currents and whisked away downstream. We then packed 9Bob, which was quite a task considering the crowd that had arrived to watch us. This was a new crowd, from a different tribe (where François had no authority), a different province and even a different time zone (the time changed in the middle of the river). We had lunch and said goodbye to François. Besides translating the needs and ideas of his fellow men into French for us, he had also been a crucial cultural adviser for us.

We explained that we had very little money left, which was true (we were not about to dip into our emergency funds), but paid him for the workers for that day. We also gave him as much as we could to cover his expenses (petrol for his motorcycle etc.) and I gave him a canoeing dry bag as a present. As we were sharing a final cup of tea with him, he asked us if we could help get his son into university in the UK. This was not the first time that someone in Africa had asked us to help get them into the UK, but it was slightly more poignant. François knew something of the outside world though his family (his father had held Belgian citizenship) and knew that a UK degree would benefit his son immensely.

Most of the people who asked us to take them with us had no idea of what the West was like, thought that everyone there lived in a paradise with endless luxuries and wealth, and believed that they would work as a labourer and live in a palace. But François had an idea, and was trying to do the best for his son. Being slightly cynical, we also wondered whether all this help had been given as a prelude to this question. Remembering Honoré, our Congolese driver friend in Cotonou, Benin, our hearts sank. While grateful for his help, it made us sad. But with François it was a moot point—there was nothing that any of us could do to help his son get into university in the UK beyond tutoring him for the scholarship tests. The reality was that François assumed that our system was like his—that it was based on who you know rather than what you know. We shook hands a final time and François got on a pirogue to the other side.

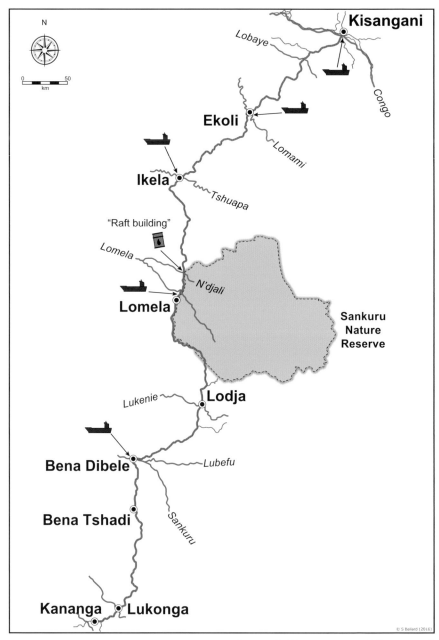

Stage 2: Kananga to Kisangani

Chapter 5

Lomela to Kisangani

Day 40: N'djali to north of Yaloketo – 30 miles
Day 41: North of Yaloketo to north of Ikela – 71 miles
Day 42: North of Ikela to GRID – 31 miles
Day 43: GRID to east of Likelonge – 40 miles
Day 44: East of Likelonge to Lomami river – 33 miles
Day 45: Lomami river to 1 mile north of Ekoli – 1 mile
Day 46: North of Ekoli to Kisangani – 101 miles

We did a set of vehicle checks and set off, back on track after nearly a week of setbacks. We drove about 500 feet before we came to a tree lying across the road. We looked at each other: had we completely misunderstood the situation on the other side of the river? Were there more problems to come? Charlie got down and inspected the tree carefully. It had been there for a while. We breathed a collective sigh of relief. As usual, people had told us that Route Nationale No.7 was clear after crossing the N'djali—which was true if your vehicle was a motorbike or bicycle. What we quickly came to realise was that the dirt track leading to Kisangani had not had any car-sized vehicle traffic on it for a long time, and so it was being reclaimed by the jungle. That afternoon, we were trying to get to a Catholic mission that we had heard was about thirty miles north of the crossing point.

Every village that we entered generated a spontaneous welcoming ceremony with kids running about and shouting and with people trying to climb on the car for the ride. They were expecting us, having heard about our struggles from the constant flow of *velo* boys. In one of the villages we stopped and talked to a few people and bought some bananas: they told us that the young people in the village had never seen a car before. The only white person they had ever seen was the priest at the mission. An older gentleman shook our hands and said he was really happy to see us—as a child, he remembered this road being a busy road, carrying traffic all day long (apparently it had been tarmacked). The destruction of the bridge during the war, and the war itself (where the N'djali river was a frontline), had completely isolated the area. He hoped that us coming along the route was a harbinger of things to come. We hoped that Alfred's road-building project would come to fruition.

It seemed to be getting dark early that evening, and then suddenly the skies opened. The rains had truly begun. Within minutes the track was inches deep in running water, and driving, I struggled to see where the track ended and the jungle began. The tyres skidded on the now wet mud and then suddenly, another bang! The front right tyre had collided with the rough end of a tree trunk, causing wood to wedge into the tyre rim where the rubber wheel joined it. As it was too wet and dark to see what we were doing we elected to continue as the tyre still had air in it. Eventually we pulled into the mission, dripping wet from the rain. We were welcomed by Toni. He had heard of us coming, of course. Apparently the whole district was talking about us. Unfortunately, the German priest was away, but we would be very welcome to stay and share supper with Toni and his colleagues. They showed us somewhere to wash and said we could sleep in the dining room. We could not have been more grateful for the dry concrete floor.

Before dinner they asked us to tell our story over fresh palm wine. As we settled down to a meal, they told us theirs. We deftly moved aside chunks of monkey spine in some of the dishes, while they explained that they mainly focused on agricultural work, and on helping the local people improve the yields of their crops. It was worthy work, except that those they helped were 'encouraged' to join the church and become active members in spreading its word. To Chloe and me, ambivalent atheists, it illustrated some of the cynicism of organised religion. Even Charlie, a relatively serious yet private Muslim, but not at all enamoured with the trappings of religious organisation, rolled his eyes. After dinner we gathered around the long-wave radio transmitter. The network of Catholic missions is one of the only things that still works country-wide in the Congo. Every evening at a designated time, all of the missions in a particular area would switch on their sets and have a conference call, sharing the news of the day. We settled down to a fitful night's sleep on the concrete floor.

The next morning, the priests served us breakfast and showed us around the grounds of the mission where they were growing all sorts of fruits and vegetables. They made our morning by giving us a custard apple and some limes—they could probably see how we needed vitamins. It was a beautiful and peaceful spot that had been a mission since the time that the Belgians were there. We changed the tyre (which was by now flat), packed up and waved goodbye to our kind hosts, then drove out of the gate past a crowd of people shouting and cheering at us, and trying to climb onto the vehicle. We hadn't realised how pleasant it had been in the mission without being on display. While it was perfectly understandable behaviour from their point of view—we had effectively come from the equivalent of Mars—it was a tiring business.

We managed to get about a quarter of a mile out of the village before Chloe, who was driving, said that she thought something was wrong. We all listened, and sure enough there was the knocking sound that she had noticed. We localised it to the rear right wheel, where we found that the axle hub was loose. It took about half an hour, during which a crowd gathered, but we jacked the car up and tightened everything up. After that we continued, hoping to make our next river crossing point—number three of five—that day.

This was a long day. We would drive a few miles and then come across a tree that had fallen across the road. We would either have to chop the tree and drag it out of the way, or try to convince some of the locals to help us, or pay them a little with perhaps a few cigarettes or chewing gum. Sometimes we would be travelling in a gully and the trunk would be about six feet off the ground. In these cases we were able to take the oil drums off the roof of the car and lower the tyre pressure to make 9Bob less tall. We would then scrape under the overhang. Other times we would have to stand on the bonnet or swing the axes over our heads to clear the tree limbs. Thankfully Charlie was strong, and I had become more so from working on the car. But none of us had significant experience in axe work, although we had learnt by watching our workers over the last few days how to chop a wedge into the trunk that you wanted to cut. It was slow work.

Alternatively, other patches of road were so narrow that we couldn't see the path for our wheels either side. Branches and grass would whip into the windows, slashing at our eyes if we'd taken our sunglasses off, and occasionally we'd hit an unseen, stiffer branch which would rip at the wheel guards or, worse, wedge in the window. The track was so narrow that it was difficult to pass the few pedestrians we encountered without pushing them into the undergrowth. On one unfortunate occasion the car caught on a tightly packed bag of red beans lashed to a bike, and they spilled out across the ground. We handed out cigarettes to the team of *velo* boys to say sorry as we scrabbled around collecting as many as possible and helping them patch their bag back up (we also paid for the beans they lost).

Our roof rack was covered in foliage, intermittently dropping pincer ants or poisonous centipedes into the car. Large locust-like grasshoppers would also jump on board—ricocheting around and thwacking us until we escorted them out. Worse still, felled trees that long ago had been cleared from the track would lie unseen in the verges. These would either dent our bumpers as they caused us to crash to a stop or spring up below the car once our front wheels had crossed them, beaching us. We had discovered that we didn't like chopping trees much, but chopping trees from underneath the car was a whole new, much trickier, problem.

The other challenge that we were to face repeatedly over this stage of the journey were the numerous partly-collapsed log bridges that crossed small streams. Once upon a time they had been part of the road network and had been maintained. Now, with no cars along this stretch of the road, they had been allowed to decay. We would walk across, trying to gauge the integrity of the rotting trunks, once or twice spotting a rusting chassis in the stream below and trying to work around the logs that had already half-fallen into the water. Sometimes we could go to the side and ford the river instead, but mostly we had to brave it.

Almost all of the bridges required reinforcement or rearrangement in some way: a tree trunk here, a lashed-on waffle board there. Again, sometimes people helped us, and other times they didn't. We were trying to save our strength as much as possible by using such people, yet we had very

little to give them. And in the Congo few people work for free. Once we were convinced we'd done all we could to reinforce the bridge, we would all play the same roles. Chloe would drive, I would do the hand signals and Charlie would keep the crowd back. For the crowd this was something new and they were genuinely caught up in the tension of whether we would or wouldn't squeeze over the precarious bridge. For our part, we became very good at judging exactly how much of a tyre we could balance on what thickness of log to hold 9Bob's weight. We only misjudged it once, which I describe later.

Later that day we came to the crossing point. We had made good progress and had covered almost sixty miles (more than the previous several days combined). There was a barge on the other side, and we signalled that we wanted to cross. As the boatman approached, we discussed our tactics. To date we had been screwed on every single crossing point, and we simply didn't have the money to spare with 200 odd miles to Kisangani. When the ferry arrived we cheerfully waved to the boatman, smiling broadly, and drove onto the boat, figuring that if he charged us a ludicrous price we would refuse to get off the boat. That is exactly what happened, with the man trying to charge us over $100 for an eighty-foot crossing. We refused, offered him $20, locked 9Bob and sat on the side of the boat, smoking.

Various negotiations were carried out, but in the end these were foreshortened because of the thirty pedestrian passengers who wanted to cross and who were pressuring the boatman not to be so greedy (knowing that whatever we paid would more than cover their own fares). As always happens in these situations, someone stepped in to mediate and within half an hour or so we were crossing the river. It didn't exactly make us feel good, but we also had very little choice. We were down to about $90, apart from an emergency reserve, which we were keeping to extract a hypothetical casualty.

As we drew up on the other side, Charlie spotted a little group of officials staring and pointing at us, practically rubbing their hands together thinking about all the bribes they would be able to extract. We were all settling into particular personality types by this point. Charlie would take a deep drag on his cigarette and roll his eyes sardonically; I would become intransigent

and visibly angry; and Chloe would remain controlled and try to reason with whoever it was that we were having problems with. Between the three of us—and occasionally we would all swap roles—we seemed to confuse the Congolese officials enough that they would let us carry on with our trip.

This group of officials was led by the DGM, so I was immediately banned from speaking to them. Charlie and Chloe went into their little hut while I parked 9Bob and fixed a couple of issues. After about twenty minutes in the hut by the river bank, they all came out and Charlie said sarcastically that they were just welcoming us and now we needed to go to their office to register. 'They are also insisting that we stay the night, because it is too dangerous to continue.'

'Yeah, but you've told them that we do this every...' Charlie cut me off. 'Obviously, and yes obviously, we've told them that we sleep in the bush every night, but they want to keep us around as long as possible so they can work out how to extract money from us.' Before I could speak again Charlie added, 'And yes, we've told them that we don't have any money and we're just travelling blah, blah. The negotiations are going just fine, don't fuck it up.' I think the others were getting annoyed with me.

Suitably chastised, I moved the Land Rover up to the office while the other two walked up with the officials. We all entered the 'office' together, which was, in fact, a bare room in an empty colonial house. There then followed the usual scene: one person would look over every page of every passport, bending to catch the light from the window, and then pass it to their senior to do exactly the same. Despite never having seen a British passport before they almost invariably refused our offer to guide them to the relevant pages. The passport would then go back to the first person so that he could begin to record the details of the passport on a form. At some point they would always ask us where we were from, reasonably enough not equating 'the United Kingdom of Great Britain and Northern Ireland' with 'l'Angleterre'. Sometimes they just settled for Ireland. Watching through the windows were scores of Congolese. The more we tried to impress on them the fact that we wanted to get going, the slower it seems that they went. We stopped saying anything; we should have learned this by now.

About halfway through they stopped talking in French to each other and switched to a dialect new to us. This was while handling my passport. From their body language we could see that they were excited. We had seen this before. They had 'discovered' a problem with the passport that they thought that they could exploit to get a bribe.

'I bet they've spotted my Republic of Congo visa and seen that it is out of date,' I said wearily. We were in the *Democratic* Republic of Congo and while the fact that these immigration officials didn't even know the name of their own country, or what their country's visa looked like in a passport, should have been funny, at that stage it wasn't. We all tried to pre-empt the inevitable situation and also to save their embarrassment by talking loudly in French between ourselves that our journey had taken us through two countries called Congo and that this Congo was better than the other one. None of them was listening to us.

'Messieurs-dames,' the *chef* began, 'there are no problems with you two,' he said, indicating Charlie and Chloe, 'but monsieur here has a visa that is out of date.'

Chloe explained, pointing out that we had identical sets of visas in our passports, and that it was a bit strange that Chloe's was ok and mine wasn't. They duly relented. By this time the conversation had moved outside and we were standing on the veranda. Once it was established that we were here legally, the deputy gave the passports back to Chloe. We could see from the *chef*'s face that he was not happy with this at all, as we were getting away. Chloe immediately put the passports in her pocket and zipped it shut. The *chef* began talking about an 'administration fee' that we must pay.

'Merci beaucoup, au revoir,' we said as we turned around and started walking back to the vehicle, as ever unwilling to pay for the good daylight driving time that they had deprived us of. The *chef* reached forward and grabbed Chloe's arm and made a move to get the passports back. I'd had enough by now and walked straight into the *chef*, pushing him backwards, shouting that it was outrageous to handle a woman like that and that he should be ashamed of himself. The crowd, ever present, swelled around us and it looked like it was about to get out of hand. Chloe took the opportunity to slip away and start 9Bob as Charlie and I slowly walked backwards to the vehicle. As soon as 9Bob started rolling forwards, Charlie and I piled in and we sped away.

A crowd half followed us as we left town, but gave up fairly quickly. It was getting dark and we needed to get some distance away to camp. We did not want to travel in the dark. It was the one golden rule that we had set ourselves and never yet broken. The 'road' was just a track as it wound its way north from Ikela, but after about fifteen minutes we found a clearing of sorts, with an old wrecked Russian-designed armoured personnel carrier from the war resting on its wheel rims in the undergrowth. It seemed as good a spot as any and we pulled up close to the vehicle and strung out hammocks between it and 9Bob. As usual we were completely exhausted and so we worked hard to get the food on, water purified and all the other necessary little jobs done.

As the food was cooking Chloe ran her regular evening clinic. Our bodies were taking the toll of the journey. Our skin was inflamed and itchy from fire ants. I had grass burns across my face and shoulders, Charlie's arm had been sliced by bamboo and everyone had cuts on their arms and legs from struggling through undergrowth. Mine were so infected that I was on a course of antibiotics. Chloe had a deep cut in her heel where a bamboo spike had pierced her flip flop. Under Chloe's guidance, I was cleaning out bits of flip flop and preparing to bandage it when we both noticed a flat white blister with a central black spot on the ball of her foot. We looked in all of our tropical medicine books, but were none the wiser. We checked each other up to the waist and found seven more of these spots on the soles and toes of Charlie's feet. I had none. I popped Chloe's and a white, very thin worm came out followed by necrotic black juice. Continuing to explore the same site, which was somehow numbed by the parasite, we found a deep cavity.

Putting dinner onto a slow cook, Chloe worked through Charlie's worm sites, excavating and cleaning them, and then bandaged them. We finally worked out that they must have come from the stream where Charlie and Chloe washed while I was away buying a new steering box in Kananga. We couldn't work out why Charlie had so many more than Chloe though, until he sheepishly admitted that he liked to bury his feet in the sandy bottom when washing in rivers 'because he liked the feeling'. That kept us laughing for a few days and reminded us of when an insect of some sort had crawled into Charlie's ear and started tickling his ear canal. This was such an intense feeling that it caused him to run around the car making a sound like he was having an orgasm. Chloe and I doubled up with laughter. Eventually Chloe had got out her auroscope and some tweezers and pulled out the offending moth.

It took a couple of weeks of regular inspections to finally clear Charlie's feet of the parasite, and Chloe kept a close watch for signs of spread such as rashes or fever. It always seemed to happen to Charlie.

The next morning we set off uneventfully. The terrain was like that of the previous day: lots of little bridges that needed repairing and bits of road that needed widening. As before we were happy to accept (and often pay for) any help offered, and usually we worked with passers-by or motorbike men in clearing the road. To be fair to them, there was absolutely no reason to keep the road clear, as the few motorbikes that passed could be pushed under or over most things. The terrain had slowly started to change, mostly due to human influence. Gone were the dense jungle and isolated villages that we had seen before the crossing of the N'djali. Rather than hunting and gathering, the villages in this area practised a slash and burn type of agriculture which often resulted in trees being felled across the roads as they were cleared out of the charred growing area. Mostly people were sympathetic to us, if a little surprised that we were passing through, and between us we managed to get the route clear.

We pulled up to one such felled tree at some point in the mid-afternoon. Looking around, there was no-one there and so we would have to tackle it ourselves. In fact, there were two trees crossing the road at head height, felled from the fields along the banks either side. Charlie grabbed an axe and jumped up on one and I started hacking at another with the machete. Chloe climbed up the bank to see if she could loosen the trunks from there.

'Oh shit,' Charlie said. 'Doctor, I've done a bad thing.'

I was about to start taking the piss out of Charlie when I looked up and saw blood spurt from his foot, quickly covering the tree he was balanced on. He had dropped the axe on his foot.

While I was scrambling up the bank towards him, Charlie reached down and clamped the wound with his fingers. He also sat down on the tree trunk, to avoid falling off. I helped him off the trunk onto the scorched bank while Chloe got the medical kit. 'That hurt, does it, mate?' Charlie was pretty pale as he lay down on the ground, still holding his foot. As with everywhere in the Congo, a few people came out of the trees at the commotion and looked at us with bemusement. We could never work out where these people came from or what they were doing: they seemed to seep out of the undergrowth.

Chloe got Charlie lying on his back, with his injured foot resting on a log, above his heart. As soon, as the pressure was released on the wound it started seeping. There was no doubt that it would need stitches and she started to lay out a mini operating theatre on the log. Charlie insisted that I get his camera so he could video himself being sewn up. I got his stuff and then also arranged for the growing audience to chop down the trees in that part of the road. They were very kind, and did it for free. This was also the day we ran out of fire—unable to buy matches anywhere since Lodja. This would be a problem for cooking, but more acutely Charlie needed a cigarette. Before Chloe could start a small child had to be sent for matches. We were surprised when he returned clutching a glowing ember from some unseen fire nearby.

Chloe had by now set up a sterile field from which to work on Charlie. After anaesthetising the foot, and with me playing nurse, wiping her brow and swatting the flies away, she cleaned and explored the wound and began to sew him up. Charlie gave up filming himself as he was starting to feel queasy. The gathered crowd quietly watched in fascination. A small child of about five or six was particularly interested and wasn't at all fazed by the blood and surgical instruments. We wondered what a British child of similar age would make of the situation. In fairly short order, Chloe had stitched Charlie up and dressed the wound. She then selected some powerful painkillers and antibiotics and explained Charlie's new regime to him. We packed up, thanked the men who had cleared the road and began on our way again. The whole routine had taken about an hour.

Charlie's injury had a massive impact on the team. Firstly, he was completely useless and in agony. He was physically the strongest member of the team and had represented the major part of the tree-chopping power. For the remainder of that afternoon, Chloe and I cleared the route, but became increasingly exhausted. Charlie was zoned-out and sat in the vehicle, high on painkillers, sharpening tools with the metal file.

It was getting to the stage where we were looking for the night's campsite when we came across a small bridge made of tree trunks lain over a stream. The track was too narrow to turn around or stop and camp in order to face it the next day. We had no choice: we had to cross the bridge. It was nothing we hadn't encountered before and we went into a well-practised sequence: Chloe began jockeying 9Bob into position while I made an inspection of the bridge to see whether it would take our weight. In a case of hope over experience, I declared it to be safe, unable to face the thought of felling more trees. It was an unfortunate decision that I got completely wrong.

Chloe mounted the bridge without mishap and got all four wheels in appropriate places to drive across. As she was slowly edging across, the bridge started to snap so I gave her the 'floor it' hand signal and jumped out of the way into dense, man-height reeds that turned out to be sharp and which lacerated my skin. Chloe managed to get 9Bob's front wheels on the other bank before bits of the bridge gave way, the rear right wheel falling about two feet and the rear axle becoming embedded on the trunks that had formerly made up the bridge. Charlie cried out in pain as the jarring shook his by-now fully unanaesthetised foot. It was starting to get dark.

Chloe pushed her way out of the car—it was hemmed in on both sides at the front by dense undergrowth. Climbing around to the back of the vehicle, we debated various options, settling at last on jacking the rear end of the car up and rebuilding/reinforcing the bridge underneath the rear wheels. Charlie whimpered in the front seat. I was completely spent by this point from clearing the route that afternoon and so Chloe had to do most of the jacking while I dealt with the inevitable crowd a lot more brusquely than I would have done had I been less tired. We all feel ashamed for the way that we dealt with some of the people we came across at various stages in the Congo; they were just curious, but in our exhaustion we were often rude. Thankfully, they were not interested in helping, and not liking being out of their villages in the dark, quickly left. Alone, we managed to get 9Bob raised and with enough supporting grip from waffle boards and tree limbs we were able to half drive, half push him out. It had taken over an hour using an original Land Rover high-lift jack, which sadly broke during the operation. By now it was completely and utterly dark. We drove forward through a path that was about a foot narrower than 9Bob looking for anywhere to sleep.

After about a mile the path widened in a small section to about two 9Bobs—not ideal, but in the circumstances it would do. We got Charlie out and put him in a chair pumping water (to purify river water we had a membrane pump) while we prepared the site. It was a terrible place to camp, with some sort of creeper foliage covering almost all the floor, so the first thing we had to do was beat the area all around the campsite with sticks to get rid of any snakes that there might have been. It felt more like being in an Indiana Jones movie than being on holiday.

We talked about trying to get Charlie to some sort of medical help— Chloe explained that he had probably broken his foot with the weight of the roughly made axe, and needed an x-ray and potentially even a surgical tendon repair. Professionally she explained his rather bleak options to him, and the possible consequences of continuing without proper medical attention. We didn't know how long it would take to get somewhere suitable for this, but Charlie bravely elected to keep going. He was in a huge amount of pain. That night, two of us slept like logs, but Charlie found it difficult.

The next day Charlie was feeling better and we pushed on. It was yet another day of small bridges and of clearing the route, one tree at a time. We were still in a part of the country where the vehicle was more interesting than the white people inside. In one village the weight of the car caused a small, unseen wooden bridge, long disguised by layers of mud, to completely collapse. In a flash, we found the back end of 9Bob in a massive hole. The villagers kindly helped us push him out by rocking the weight onto the wheels that still had traction. People were kinder here, and even the transport of chickens was more humane—carrying them in little wicker briefcases rather than upside down tied by their feet to handlebars. We no longer saw pigs screaming for their lives, frothing at the mouth, tied to the back of bikes either.

We were starting to come into the orbit of Kisangani and the *velo* boys whom we spoke to (an amazing source of route information) said that it took a week to get into Kisangani to get supplies. They then came back to sell their goodies in the villages nearby. We even found a whole family walking back from Kisangani, where they had gone to attempt to resolve a dispute with the government (to no avail). We knew that we were getting to the end of this section and we were thankful. It had been tougher than we could have possibly imagined. That afternoon, seeing the end in sight, we hired a young man to sit on the bonnet of 9Bob with an axe and a machete and help us clear the route. We felt a bit uncomfortable asking him to do it, but he seemed happy enough and we didn't have much choice—Charlie was still out of action, and Chloe and I were shattered. He stayed with us for hours and probably helped us cross ten miles or more.

That evening we slept in a health centre that was still being constructed by USAID. Its manager was really kind and found us rattan beds which we sank onto wearily. For once Chloe ran her evening clinic in a proper medical setting rather than in the bush. We had covered forty miles that day.

The next morning we had a lie-in and a big breakfast. Today we hoped to make the penultimate crossing before Kisangani over the River Lomami, a major tributary of the River Congo. Brutally, this was one of the hardest days of route clearing and small bridge crossing. As an added bonus we had to deal with several sections of subsided track; for the first time we nearly lost the car down a slope. In this particular section of the obstacle course what appeared to be a track only wide enough for a motorbike was indeed a track only wide enough for a motorbike, with sheer banks either side hidden by foliage. Inevitably, the car finally slipped in the mud, with the back end swinging round and crashing through sapling trees. Each time we tried to edge forward the back end slipped further round, the front right wheel with traction on the path forming the turning point. This was it. If the car fell down, then even with the winch there'd be little chance of getting it up and out of the muddy hole. Recruiting villagers to hang with me onto the left side of the vehicle and rocking the wheel into contact with the ground, we managed to edge back onto the path.

After a long, long day, we found the Lomami, but the barge had been out of action for many years. Its huge hulk sat rusting on the opposite bank, home to several families. The Lomami is huge—nearly 1000 feet wide—and fast-flowing. The thought of building a raft with which we could paddle across it was madness. We spoke to several people and they showed us a road that went along the river bank for a few miles that took us to a crossing point opposite a town called Ekoli. The road was akin to a swamp and in several places we had to place bamboo over the worst sections to give us traction.

At last we pulled up to a clearing on the bank which many moons ago had been a concrete wharf and jetty area. Nowadays it was just a grassy slope. Across the other side we could see Ekoli, but as it was only a couple of hours before nightfall we decided to have a relaxing evening washing ourselves and eating our last tin of sardines with some rice. We added a little interest to our diet by nibbling and sucking on palm nuts given to us by some children—they tasted of a cross between brazil nuts and avocado and stained our fingers and lips orange. We gathered lots of wood and made a big fire, chatting to some men who told us that we needed to talk to the *chef* on the other side about crossing, and that they had made rafts before for officials with cars. We had only covered thirty-three miles that day.

We got up early. Charlie was beginning to feel better now and we were in good spirits. To be sure, crossing the Lomami was not going to be easy, but like other problems we had faced, we were pretty sure we could do it. I set across the river in a pirogue after negotiating the price with the boatman. I took with me a jar of dates that we had carried with us since Mauritania, reasoning that we might as well try and throw everything into what was inevitably going to be a difficult negotiation. These pirogues were significantly bigger and more robust than those we'd seen before, carrying up

to fifteen people at a time, and not likely to be sunk by the several motorbikes that piled in. We landed on a little beach on the other bank, jostling with pirogues and with young boys hopping from boat to boat. There was a bustling, market feel. I paid my fare and was directed over to the *chef*'s hut.

Outside was an old man sitting down surrounded by many younger men who were standing up. I waited until I had the chief's attention and explained in my best, politest French (which was still pretty rough) that we were travelling from England, needed to cross the Lomami and I was hoping that the *chef* would be able to help out. As I spoke, I handed over the dates and explained that they had come from Mauritania. The chief couldn't have looked less interested, took the dates and put them on the floor. Barely even looking at me, he said, 'five hundred dollars'.

I had been expecting some sort of difficulty over the crossing, and, of course, there was going to be a discussion about the price. But how much? It was difficult to know what to say. I tried again, saying that we were just travellers and were poor, and that we didn't have five hundred dollars. The chief shrugged and started talking to someone else. That was the deal, he seemed to be saying. Take it or leave it. How great was I at negotiating? I wandered off through the huts, wondering what to do. Eventually I bumped into an old man and stopped to talk to him.

After a brief description of the situation, the old man took my hand and led me back to the chief. An argument ensued which I couldn't follow, but the body language was fairly clear. The man was advocating on our behalf and the chief still wasn't interested. Finally I was invited to present my price, and as we only had $80 left I said $50. This was not at all acceptable and the chief wouldn't move at all. I decided to deploy the raft card and mentioned that we had already crossed a river by building a raft and we would do it again here. 'Fine,' said the chief. Game, Set and Match.

I thanked the old man and headed back to the pirogue. One of the young retainers detached himself from the crowd and followed me, getting into the boat that was crossing. Taking this as a signal that the *chef* was still open to negotiation, I tried again. The man then began to barter with me, moving away from the flat statement that it was $500 or nothing. I had no idea whether the man had the authority for this, but there was nothing to lose.

The negotiations continued on the far bank and for good measure we got all the oil drums down from the 9Bob's roof and started laying them out as if to prepare for making a raft. This had a slightly different effect to the one intended and the man took it that we were crossing by our own raft, got in a pirogue and left. We looked at each other, not sure what to do. Through not really having enough money and/or negotiating too harshly, we had boxed ourselves into a corner. None of us wanted to cross this massive river by raft—it would be significantly more challenging than the N'djali, but we couldn't persuade the officials to take us for a price that we could pay. Wearily, we organised some workers and set off into the forest to look for *tshumbe* trees.

After about an hour we hadn't found any *tshumbe* and so we had a rethink. Chloe decided that it was worth having another go with the chief, and taking our $80, all our remaining francs and some leftover Liberian dollars for good measure, headed over the river in a pirogue. She took a slightly different tack, saying that I was mad and that I wanted to cross the river in a raft. She told them that she thought it was too dangerous and that we would all die, but that I was like a crazy man trying to build this raft. She couldn't control me, she said. There was some truth in the story. In essence, in a highly misogynistic society she played the female card. It worked. They agreed to build us a raft based on lashed-together pirogues for $80 plus our remaining francs. She handed over the money, they inspected it and the deal was shaken on. We hoped we would reach Kisangani soon as we could no longer buy food and we were running out. Go Chloe!

Things then started to happen. The residents of Ekoli clearly did this very often and they set to work quickly gathering the spars used to lash three of the sturdy pirogues together. Within an hour they were nearly complete and we lent them our oil drums to make it yet more stable. Literally, just as we were about to drive on someone came over from the other side and spoke to the foreman. We couldn't cross as three of our twenty dollar bills were *déchiré* or in some way not in mint condition.

We had come across this problem before, but the bills we had given over were fairly new and smart, and they had inspected them before agreeing the deal. We couldn't quite work out whether they believed us that we had no more money. Our emergency money was in crisp one hundred dollar bills, but we couldn't risk breaking into it, not knowing what lay ahead. Besides, we had sworn blind that we only had $80 left. They kept on asking us to change the bills and we were not sure whether they were pushing to see if we had more money. It is a fairly common negotiating tactic to let deals almost go through and then pull back at the last minute in order to try and get more money. We stuck to our guns, but they were adamant that they couldn't accept the bills. We tried to substitute oil drums for money, but they weren't interested. An increasingly bad-tempered argument ensued, the rules of business or even honour seemingly irrelevant. They began to deconstruct the raft.

While Chloe and I tried to slow them down as much as possible, Charlie went back across the river, this time to find the chief of police. Surely the officials must have some use. Apparently they were stationed five miles away, but instead he found the greedy old chief. In the event the chief didn't give a damn about the agreement, but he was annoyed that we were calling his associates thieves. He came back across with Charlie on a pirogue, overruled the foreman and told him that he had to accept three oil drums and the $20 note that was deemed acceptable. We were finally on our way again. This was the last river that we thought we might need to raft across, so it actually worked out well swapping money for drums.

Once the raft had been reconstructed we loaded 9Bob onto it and cast off. It barely dipped in the water: this was a proper raft unlike the one we had built. This time, due to the width of the river, we had a troop of oarsmen lined up on both sides of the raft paddling in sync to the rhythm of a song. The chief stood on the raft surveying them and shouting at them to work harder as we carved an arc in the river, first paddling upstream and then drifting down into the other bank taking advantage of the fast current in the middle of the river.

Once we got to the other side there was absolute chaos with hundreds of people mobbing the sandy landing area trying to get a look at us. The dock area was covered in rusting shipping hulks from the Belgian era and half-destroyed concrete jetties. This had clearly been a major transhipment point to get resources out of the interior. Chloe and Charlie focused on getting 9Bob ready for the journey ahead while I organised the recovery of the oil drums and ropes from the raft. I handed over the three best oil drums in payment, and began coiling the rope. One of the ropes had gone missing. We refused to move from the dockside and threatened to call the chief down again unless the rope was returned. After a bit of a standoff it was returned by the foreman. They looked like they wanted us gone. The feeling was mutual. Registration with the DGM was for once quick and simple, and the official was not upset when we declined the offer of paying him for his services. As we drove away we tried to find a shop to buy some cigarettes, but were told that the town did not have a single shop. Whether this was true or whether they just wanted to see the back of us, we didn't know. We drove about a mile up the road, which was wide and made of compacted sand, and pulled off to the side to camp (locals had previously eulogised the road quality on this stretch as 'la pureté de la pureté'). We had one hundred miles to go until Kisangani.

We got up the next morning as early as possible and whizzed through our morning routine. There was a reasonable chance that we could be sleeping in a bed in Kisangani that night after a cold beer. The road was mostly good, and everyone we spoke to said that the journey was easily possible in a day. Although we had heard this sort of thing before we still allowed our hopes to rise. Yesterday had slightly crushed our belief in the human spirit.

Big muddy holes were a new road feature, but we only had to dig ourselves out once that day. The main concern was trying to get fuel; we hadn't seen any diesel since Lodja, and the rough roads and tree dragging had not been conducive to fuel economy. Our worries were somewhat lessened by seeing another car for the first time since Mr White Shirt's in Lomela. Unfortunately it was an ancient Land Cruiser stuck in a stream bed. The driver had chosen to brave the water rather than balance across the rotting log bridge. Faced with no other route, we carefully edged across

and then reversed to pull the Land Cruiser out. Its passengers thanked us and reassured us we would find some roadside fuel soon. We were feeling optimistic despite the fact that 9Bob seemed to be steering to the right, and so to drive straight we had to constantly steer to the left. Although we only noticed it that day, it had probably been the case for several days and we just hadn't managed to get any speed up. He also had a limp, we later found out due to a smashed radial arm bush. We decided to leave it and try to sort it out in Kisangani.

We made good time and thankfully found some men with bottles of diesel beside the road. After some back and forth while they tried to convince us that the four-litre mark on their five-litre container in fact represented five litres (maybe they really believed this) we settled on a price. They were unconcerned by our previously-rejected $20 bills and gave us change in francs, meaning we were able to stop in a little roadside shack for lunch (caterpillars and *feuillage*).

We were very much out of the jungle now and firmly in the orbit of Kisangani. Practically every village along the road had a sign advertising development projects of various sorts—the Lomami river seemed to be the limit of how far they went, although there had been a couple of exceptions like the health clinic near the N'djali. We had found similar-sized zones of development influence (about a hundred miles) around most big towns in the Congo. Just after lunch we came to our penultimate crossing. We expected the worst, but the boat captain came to us, welcomed us and asked for $30, showing us his official price list and receipt book. To get the money we sold our remaining three oil drums and rope to a trader gaining a slight profit on what we had bought them for 450 miles ago.

A smooth crossing later, and a friendly wave from the captain, and we were off, driving the last few miles into Kisangani. Following a police checkpoint, we were stopped by the secret service, who nearly became the first officials to successfully extract money from us by putting 9Bob through an on-the-spot roadside MOT. You had to hand it to their imagination: 9Bob was in a parlous state after what he had been through. Bizarrely, the headlights only came on when braking, a problem we'd noticed during routine checks a few days ago. Lashings from bamboo branches had lost us bulbs, but we had just enough intact to technically pass. We gave them the best light show we could, and by convincing them that some of the lights were for decoration rather than for safety, and then showing them our UK MOT certificate from a garage in Oxfordshire (!), they let us through, disappointed. Luckily, they were only interested in the front lights and knew little about road safety. A third of a mile beyond the checkpoint we came to the final river crossing: we were back at the River Congo. Across the river we could see Kisangani proper. A large ferry, running to a formal timetable with a polite team quoting honest prices, carried us across.

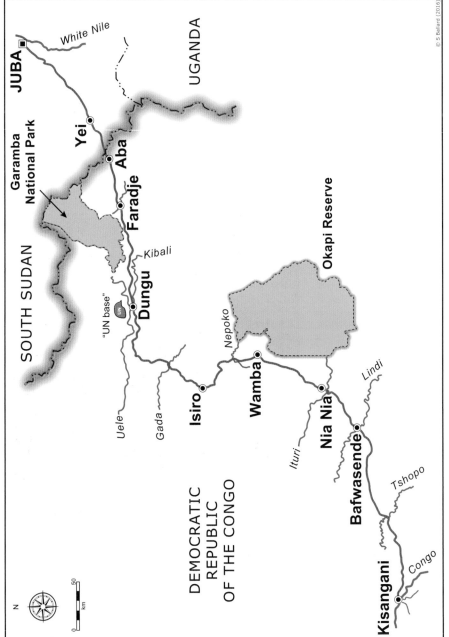

Stage 3: Kisangani to Juba

© S Ballard (2016)

Chapter 6

Kisangani to Juba

Day 47-48: Kisangani
Day 49: Kisangani to Mandjoho – 68 miles
Day 50: Mandjoho to east of Bafwagbouma – 118 miles
Day 51: E. of Bafwagbouma to N. of Bombombi – 104 miles
Day 52: North of Bombombi to Isiro – 69 miles
Day 53: Isiro to Niangazi – 26 miles
Day 54: Niangazi to Niangara – 79 miles
Day 55: Niangara to Dungu – 67 miles
Day 56-7: Dungu – 23 miles
Day 58: Dungu to north of Laso (South Sudan) – 136 miles
Day 59: North of Laso to Gange Payam – 36 miles
Day 60: Gange Payam to Juba – 44 miles

Arriving in Kisangani was something of a shock after the last three weeks. It had the first bank machines since Kinshasa, and the first Wi-Fi. There were plenty of mosques and the culture felt a lot more Muslim than that which we had experienced to date. In centuries past, Europeans and East African Muslim slavers had fought over Kisangani. It was an important port at the highest navigable point on the Congo river, some 1300 miles from its mouth. We managed to get a place to sleep in church accommodation—we don't know what we would have done in the Congo without the various churches to house us. After washing we went out for a meal; I fell asleep before the food came. We tried to go on the internet but it was woefully slow. We went to bed.

The next morning we allowed ourselves a lie in. Once we had eaten breakfast (croissants and bread, such luxury) we stood in a little huddle around 9Bob looking at his sorry state. Poor, poor 9Bob. All but one of the wheel arch mudguards had been ripped off, and his bodywork was scratched and dented everywhere. The front bumper was twisted in a grim half smile, an air vent bent out of place, a wing mirror cracked. Half the electrics didn't work. The wheel hubs were loose and he was still steering to the right. There was a suspicious knocking again now we were on tarmac, probably related to the front prop-shaft. The radiator was leaking and various belts, oils and gizmos needed changing. One of our six tyres was still out of action. He was a total mess and we couldn't really afford to have him breaking down on us over the next, and final, leg of our trip.

This part of the Congo was host to various rebel groups, including some groups of the Lord's Resistance Army (LRA). They had been chased out of Uganda recently and were hiding in the jungle in the area between South Sudan, Congo and Uganda. They kept themselves alive and fed by hijacking vehicles and kidnapping the occupants to porter the contents of the vehicle to their jungle hideouts. They had not had the opportunity to capture foreigners to date, so we were unsure whether we would get the same treatment. Just in case, when we victualled the car we over-filled it with food, very obviously on display so that there would be lots for them to take. We also hid some backup food and various communications devices in the bodywork so that we would have something to come back to after a jungle trek. We devised an action plan as to what we would do if we were stopped, and if we were kidnapped.

First we had to get 9Bob going. Slightly daunted by the scale of the challenge, we slowly walked around and made a list of all the jobs we needed to do. Just cleaning and overhauling everything would take several hours. We spent the rest of that day doing what we could with the resources that we had and trying to figure out the weird steering problem. We finally tracked it down to the tracking rod being bent out of shape, and with it a cracked tie bar. The burst bush on the radial arm only worsened the problem. When we accelerated it allowed the right front wheel to move further back with respect to the chassis (all the wheels are able to move independently with respect to the chassis on a Land Rover) so that the car veered off in one direction. The off-steering had also damaged the cupola in the wheel ball joint, which by a complete fluke was one of the spares that we had carried since England. That explained the clunking.

Unfortunately, we didn't have any of the right size bushes or any of the electrical components.

I also checked in with the embassy. Our contact there had been starting to wonder where we had got to and was uncertain what to tell the ambassador. I told him the story about Lomela and the arrest, which seemed to brighten up his day. I told him our timetable going forward and arranged our next check-in point. To have him looking out for us was an enormous psychological safety net for which we were very grateful. We also got in touch with the British Army officer who was serving with the UN in Dungu. He gave us a quick security brief on the phone about the route that we would take to Dungu. He invited us to stay a night with him, which was an absolute blessing—we wouldn't be able to camp rough in this area as we had done before since we thought that we would make ourselves too much of a target.

That night Chloe and I went to a hotel in Kisangani to use the Wi-Fi. Rather grimly, we had to email our wedding venue and cancel the booking. We also emailed all of our international guests and told them, just in case they were planning to book flights. We'd agreed not to tell anyone that we'd actually split up though—it would have been too much worry for them with us so far away. Chloe also had to ring the UK to block her bank card which had been cloned in Nigeria and used to empty her account. It was a weird reminder that soon this would all be over—soon we wouldn't have enough resources to continue whether we had the will or not. All we had to do was cross the last 800 miles of the Congo.

The next day we got up early and went to Kisangani's market. After asking around we were directed to a garage that, like many garages in Africa, had a massive spare parts scrapyard next to it. Claude, the chief mechanic, listened patiently and led us to the scrapyard, where there was a Range Rover sitting on blocks. A quick check underneath revealed some bushes that, with a bit of reshaping, would be fine. He also explained how to fix our radiator using a mix of glue and sand to make a plaster-like substance to stop it leaking. We managed to pick up everything else in the market and returned back to the church where we worked on 9Bob for as long as the light held out and then by torchlight. We crawled into bed having managed to complete most of our tasks.

We only managed to set off the next day in the early afternoon after stocking the car with food and fuel and thoroughly cleaning and repairing everything that we could. At least in Kisangani we'd been able to find pasta for the first time in a long time, as well as luxuries such as tomato paste, Laughing Cow cheese and chocolate spread. As we departed the city we had a blazing row with the checkpoint guards who tried to get us to pay a bribe to leave. My behaviour was getting worse and worse. In the end we managed to play the multiple government agencies stationed at the checkpoint (army, intelligence, roads etc.) against each other by whipping up public 'moral' outrage at the fact that the intelligence service had asked us for a bribe, even though they all habitually took bribes. This was starting to get tiring.

The road, however, was excellent. Tarmac quickly gave way to compressed gravel, but there was space for two lanes and plenty of traffic. We sped along and by the end of the day we had covered over seventy miles. We spent the night in a village after asking the headman. We had never felt the need before, but with the LRA (and there were some other random groups as well, such as the Allied Democratic Forces, an Islamist group allied to Al-Shabaab in Somalia) we thought it was better to be safe than sorry. This part of the road was also fairly well travelled. Chloe had an unidentified fever, but the night was otherwise uneventful.

We woke that morning to ladies speaking and singing in tongues in the wood and straw church by our tent. The next day was much the same as before except that at some point the rear right suspension coil snapped with a loud twang. This was an interesting problem, and there was not much that we could do about it: we had lost about a quarter of the length of the coil. We jacked the car up and removed the broken part of the spring and then inverted it so that it sat properly in its place. We then repacked the car to put heavier things on the left until the car body looked like it was roughly level. As the day wore on the road quality started to deteriorate due to a combination of very heavy rains and still fairly busy traffic (in this part of the world that was one vehicle every five minutes).

At first we were able to traverse the water-filled, 9Bob-sized holes in the road with a combination of speed and luck. But then we understood the meaning of the warning we had been given in Kisangani that the trucks had a tendency to block the road: they became stuck in the holes, causing massive queues of vehicles going back both ways. As the only thing that could pull a lorry out was another lorry, it often took a bit of time to get everything lined up to get the first lorry out. Often the wire tow cables snapped, necessitating the involvement of yet more trucks. In the meantime the hole would be filled with tree branches and other debris for traction, and lots of digging would take place. Each lorry carried a crew of young men for the purpose. Some of the queues we encountered had been there for three to four days. The problem was that each time a lorry was stuck the hole would get deeper, and each time it rained the depth of the hole, and the bits of wood thrown in, would be hidden. Apparently a Chinese firm had been contracted three years earlier to build the road properly, but every time they pisted it, the rains would come, a lorry would get stuck and the surface would gradually be dug up again. In the end the Chinese refused to proceed while the digging continued.

There was little discipline in the queues, and smaller vehicles would often try to push past, thereby blocking the exit route for the embedded lorry. The exception was one place where a lone Congolese policeman was trying to organise the queue. Where he came from we had no idea. In all other places it was a question of collecting enough people together who felt that a sense of order should prevail and then pressuring the queue breakers into accepting that order. In some cases I would get into their vehicles and move them out of the way while others physically held the drivers back. It was an interesting lesson in how to conduct democracy in a society where there was absolutely no trust, the lack of which generated much selfish behaviour. Of course, we say that now, but at the time it was maddening.

There was mostly a good atmosphere at these sites, and we would sit around drinking tea and joking with the lorry drivers, many of whom were Ugandan (and so spoke English). Disturbingly, at a couple of sites leery comments were made about Chloe by local men. In one case I pushed a man into a muddy hole because he felt it appropriate to describe what he wanted to do to her. This caused much merriment amongst the surrounding crowd and the comments stopped. More than anywhere else in the world that any of us had experienced, in the Congo the strong prevailed over the weak. We also encountered unprecedented levels of *schadenfreude*. The Congolese, in our experience, loved nothing more than to laugh at other people's misfortune. We felt we needed to be tough and strong, and critically, to act tough and strong—just to get through. Perhaps it was the siege mentality of the journey, but we always trod a fine line between what worked and what was going too far.

Just as it was starting to get dark and we were looking for a place to camp, we came up to a massive tailback. The hole in the road was as deep as the lorry stuck in it and two or three times as long. We think that the hole originally appeared because the road had been built over a river without a proper culvert. The river was now emptying into the hole, making it a lake. It was ludicrous. In addition to trucks trying to pull each other out, some enterprising Congolese villagers had hacked a bypass through the jungle to one side. It had been built up to take it above the water level and was quite an impressive feat of engineering considering that the villagers only had their shovels and hands with which to create it. Of course, and this was fair enough, they were charging people to go over it, which in some cases required them pulling the vehicle by hand up the hill if it couldn't make it under its own steam. Amazingly given the road conditions, there were several family sedans: the road took you to Bunia and thence to Uganda. We had seriously contemplated running along this road and escaping to Uganda, but we had heard that some of the fighting in the east had displaced various armed groups into the vicinity of Bunia.

We waited in the queue for hours. It would move forward several hundred yards and then another lorry would become stuck and the whole saga would start again. Eventually, as we neared the front, a double-articulated lorry found itself stuck in the hole, meaning that no single lorry was powerful enough to pull it out. We were able to line up to go through the track that had been hacked out of the jungle and, with it appearing to be clear, we quickly drove up it after establishing that we would pay the same $5 as everyone else, especially since we didn't need pulling. Speed was essential—we'd seen other cars pause on the precarious mud bridge and slowly slip backwards, or worse sideways, off the narrow causeway.

Unfortunately, a team of pullers started to haul a Vauxhall Zafira from the other end at the same time and we met about two-thirds of the way along (from our end). A fearsome argument ensued, but it was our fault: we should have checked. Very carefully, we reversed down the track with Chloe driving and Charlie and I carefully inspecting the edge of the track where began a muddy slope straight into the hole. Doing this in the pitch black by torchlight, with a cacophony of people shouting and engine noise going on around us, was nerve wracking.

Once we had reversed off the track our bad behaviour had earned us an increase in the 'toll'. This took another half an hour to negotiate back down to the original level. Tempers were frayed on all sides. Finally, at about 2 am, we passed over the obstacle and drove a further mile until we found a road-building quarry from which the gravel to make the road had been extracted. We slept soundly. We had made 118 miles that day.

The next day we woke still covered head-to-toe in mud. We were making good time and we didn't want to rush into a rebel-held zone so we had a lazy breakfast and wet wiped ourselves. The roads seemed to improve after we left the main route at Nia Nia: fewer lorries meant fewer holes. We passed through an Okapi reserve and kept careful lookout. The Okapi is an exceptionally rare animal only found wild in this one reserve in the entire world: related to the giraffe, it looks like a horse, but its legs are striped like a zebra. The generations of war in the Congo had meant that, like many of the local species including the White Rhino, it had been hunted almost to extinction. The rarity meant that people came from all over the world to try to get a glimpse, but our chances of spotting one from the road were somewhere around zero. As we drove, the landscape was changing again, with tall rainforest trees creating vistas of never-ending green.

Around mid-afternoon we were stopped at a police checkpoint by a log dragged across the road. At first wary that it might be some sort of trap— we hadn't seen any checkpoints since leaving Kisangani—we approached slowly and, putting the car in reverse, left the engine running. Two men in police uniform who had been lying on a tatty mattress at the side of the road ambled over.

'Vous entrez une zone rouge,' the tall one began. 'Vous faites quoi ici?'

'Une zone rouge, monsieur?' we replied, thinking that this was the usual prelude to a demand for money. 'Why is it une zone rouge?'

'Because there are very dangerous armed pygmies in the forests,' he countered, 'this is the most dangerous place in the world for armed pygmies.' We looked at each other. We had been expecting something about the LRA, the Islamist terrorists or the various rebel groups engaged in the war in the east. Playing along, we asked how it was that pygmies could be so dangerous, given their stature. To make the point Charlie squatted down, pretending to hold a rifle. We'd seen pygmies on the road, pictures of stoicism with their heavy loads hanging down their backs from straps across their foreheads. They were extremely shy, melting into the trees as the car approached.

'We are not worried about pygmies, monsieur; we are worried about the LRA. Where are they?'

'There are no LRA here at all,' he said, repeating a refrain that we were to hear repeatedly over the next few days. He then launched into a long description of pygmy raiding parties coming in from the forest and attacking villages. The idea of three-foot jungle raiders was too much for us and the five of us burst out laughing. Slowly we realised that the red-eyed policemen were laughing much harder than us—one of them had started to cry with laughter—and it dawned on us that they were completely stoned.

Once we had got them back on track they wanted to register us in a hardback police record book. Good naturedly, they took our passports and, accepting our help in deciphering them, entered the details in the ledger. While this was going on a young woman walked past with children and a bowl of agricultural produce on her head. Without even breaking the conversation, one of the policemen walked over and accepted the proffered note. We were visibly uncomfortable watching the transaction, and the woman picked up on our unease. She looked at us and shrugged as if to say, 'Welcome to my life.' This unspoken communication was completely missed by the policemen who had descended into fits of giggles again.

Having entered our details, there was a half-hearted attempt to extract a bribe from us. As per usual, this was flatly refused and the two policemen began arguing with each other about whether it was appropriate to try to extract a bribe from us. We let them get on with it, pulled the log out of the way and drove off, with them standing by the mattress staring at us. We don't think anyone had done that to them before. We still do not know if they were being serious about the armed pygmies.

The road quality was deteriorating again, and we repeatedly found ourselves in ditches filled with knee-deep liquid mud, so viscous that ants could walk on it. The bottoms of the ditches were soft and provided no traction. It turned out that there were still a few lorries around, but to our horror they were a smaller version of the orange mining type. Again the ruts they created beached us, but this time the target for our digging was often under half a foot of slime. We tried to take small detours where possible yet we were pretty hemmed in by jungle. Villages were further apart, but sometimes their inhabitants would kindly offer to let us pass through their yard space to avoid a hole or a bogged-down lorry.

In one sad incident we heard that a child had been killed a week previously when a truck had passed between two houses to avoid a hole. To avoid the same hole we had unknowingly asked to do the same, as usual approaching on foot to check that there was a suitable route. We were met by an (understandably) hysterical man who lay down across the path when he saw 9Bob. No amount of explaining, reasoning or begging could persuade him to move. Respecting his wishes, we finally entered the hole, inevitably becoming stuck. We spent the next forty-five minutes digging ourselves out while trying to ignore driving instructions from people who had never sat in a car before.

We spent that night in another road-building quarry. This was to be our last night sleeping out: from then on we would stay in buildings or with people to attempt to mitigate the rebel threat. We were always at our most vulnerable when we were all asleep at night, and we wanted to avoid having to sleep with a sentry again. When we were in Kisangani we had downloaded onto our notebook as much information as possible about the LRA and north-east Congo: that night we reviewed it in the quarry. It told us nothing that would help us protect ourselves.

The next day we got up early as we had to make it to the town of Isiro, seventy miles further on, in order to avoid camping out. Approaching the mud pits, everything was done as fast as possible. 9Bob would be brought to a halt about thirty feet before a hole and Chloe or I (Charlie's foot could still not be submerged) would jog out with a stick that was used to probe the water-filled pit. Once we had determined its depth and the best route through, the person on the ground would guide the driver. Even so, we were bogged in fairly regularly. For the first time in the entire six months we used the winch to pull ourselves out, anchored against a massive tree. Charlie's enthusiasm at having a physically active task again as well as his general strength and determination quickly earned him the nickname 'General Winch'.

Getting bogged in was approached in an aggressive fashion: we did not want to hang around for too long in any one place. Local villagers could sometimes be drafted in to push, shovel and clear; we would winch, reinforce and manoeuvre. Once, in frustration, I even attempted to push 9Bob out of

a hole of deep water on my own, face planting in the stinking mud when Chloe's driving skills meant the wheels got purchase on the ground, much to the amusement of Charlie and Chloe. It was an adrenaline-filled day.

We finally pulled into Isiro with both us and the vehicle looking like we had been spray-blasted with mud. Isiro is a reasonably sized town, with Belgian red-brick, tin-roofed buildings, a couple of hotels and Chinese goods in the shops. We were immediately identified by the DGM official, who then followed us around and finally helped us find a suitable hotel. According to his records, the last time Isiro saw tourists was in 2008. The Muslim hotel owners were lovely, and Charlie, who was Muslim, went to the local mosque with the owner's son to celebrate *Iftar* (fast breaking)—it was Ramadan. Taking advantage of the running water and light, Chloe removed Charlie's stiches that evening.

The next morning we looked around Isiro trying to find a replacement for our broken suspension coil. As in most Congolese towns, there was a network of garages and spare part merchants, and we were directed to a garage set in an old colonial building. The mechanics did have a selection of springs but wanted more money for them than we could pay (over $200), so we left without fixing the spring. After a quick lunch we headed north on the road to a mission that we had been pointed to only twenty-six miles away. Ideally we wanted to go further than this, but we had to break our journey into one-day hops between 'safe' locations. The roads were utterly deserted and we felt very vulnerable.

About five miles out of Isiro, we became horribly bogged in, and only managed to get out by winching, pushing, digging and waffle boarding all at the same time. We managed to get out of the hole and, before we had even put the equipment away, got bogged in again. Bemused villagers stood around and laughed at us. This time a submerged sheet of metal cut a huge gash in the sidewall of the front-right tyre. We half-dragged ourselves out of the hole and, due to another massive hole six feet further on, changed the tyre in a foot of liquid mud by using the waffle boards to create a platform upon which to jack the car. Doing this while looking over our shoulders the whole time was not nice, and we changed the tyre in about three minutes.

It was starting to feel like we were leading 9Bob over an obstacle course again. Every so often the slime-filled bogs would give way to deeply gullied, chassis-twisting, rocky terrain.

In the late afternoon we pulled up at the enormous Catholic mission in Niangazi. Desperately in need of some Christian kindness, we were warmly welcomed by the portly priests inside. They gave us a tour and, leaving our car in the former stable blocks, offered us a room. They also pointed out the bathroom where they would bring a bucket of hot (hot?!) water to wash. Bliss. We did the absolute minimum that we had to do to the vehicle (cleaning the windows so we could see out of them, etc.) and moved our sleeping stuff into the room. We washed in hot water, which was a spiritual experience, and then sat down outside the refectory with an aperitif (an aperitif?!) in our hands. It was then that they delivered the killer line.

'We think it is fair that you pay $100 to stay here.'

They had not even hinted at money before. We had approached them and simply asked to camp within their yard—they had then shaken their heads and insisted on what they called hospitality. Wearily, we repeatedly reiterated that we'd be happy to camp, we just needed security. Considering that it cost $10 a head to stay in the middle of Kinshasa (albeit with the entire DRC cycling team), they were taking advantage. Eventually, after threatening to leave altogether, we settled on about $25. Perhaps $100 doesn't sound much, and we knew that when we recounted this story later once we got home people would be aghast at our stinginess, but we were short of cash, having spent everything on keeping 9Bob going. More to the point, we were sick to the back teeth of being ripped off and being seen as cash registers because we were foreigners. Once we had settled the money, the conversation moved onto more pleasant matters and we moved inside to have dinner around a long, wooden dinner table.

The next morning we awoke before dawn and prepared 9Bob in the dark. We had over eighty miles to cover that day to Niangara, the geographic centre of the African continent. If the roads were anything like yesterday, it was going to be a long, hard day. We were warming the engine and finishing

off our coffee as the first hint of light entered the compound. Waving goodbye and thanking the priests, we pulled away. The roads were much like before, and we quickly dirtied ourselves in the puddles of mud. In many cases these even reached over the height of the exhaust and we had to make sure that we had a clear run out of each hole because water travelling up the exhaust pipe would rapidly spell the end of our jaunt. We took it in turns to reconnoitre the holes, gauging their depth and plotting paths through. We worked quickly with some expectation in our minds—in a matter of days, if all went well, we would be in South Sudan, and safe.

That day we ate a cold lunch, scrounging what we had to hand in the car as we didn't want to take the time to stop. A few minutes after lunch we were forced to take a diversion around a horrendous dip in the road down a small bypass that had been cleared out of the forest. As we pulled back onto the road we heard a crack that seemed to come from 9Bob. Pulling the car over, we got out. The roof rack had collapsed and was resting on the roof of the car. It had collided with low-leaning bamboo branches one too many times. Not pausing, we rearranged our kit in the back and managed to fit nearly everything that had been in the roof rack inside the car. We also took the opportunity to ditch the rack, our one surviving camp chair and various spare parts/boxes/ropes/ extra kit that we had been carrying—with the spring damaged on the right hand side, we wanted to keep the weight as low as possible.

While we were completing the reorganisation of the vehicle and strapping the waffle boards directly to the roof of the vehicle a group gathered around us. We briefly explained that we were tourists and that we were travelling through the Congo and carried on with our work. They then carried on talking about us in French, which in itself was unusual, but perhaps their mother tongues were different and so they were using French to communicate. Eavesdropping on their conversation, it was only at this point that it became clear that in their vocabulary the word 'tourist' meant 'someone who comes to the Congo to exploit its natural resources'. What was a 'tourist'?

'It's a foreigner who comes here looking for minerals,' they said. It suddenly all fell into place—the hassle, the jeering, the situation in Lomela, the 'knowing' looks—'tourist' in the Congo meant something completely different, all those unscrupulous individuals who had come to pillage had pretended they were 'tourists'. We were a bunch of complete idiots: we had spent the entire journey telling everyone that we were tourists, without realising why people responded negatively. And of course there were no actual tourists: nobody would be so stupid as to come here on holiday. Every day in the Congo was like peeling an onion, where with each layer of skin that we removed we learned more about ourselves, and more about the Congo. But we barely scratched the surface of the Congo. We drove off, sitting in a quiet contemplative silence, marvelling at our ignorance.

We arrived at Niangara still in silence. Lots of semi-derelict red-brick buildings stood back from the road, with mud huts dotted in-between. It was a quiet, one-road town. Yet because it was on the east-west UN supply route from Uganda (and eventually Kenya and the sea), it contained a fair few NGOs. It also had a monument, erected by the Belgians, celebrating the town as the geographical centre of Africa. We were probably about two days from the border with South Sudan along a long, straight, UN-maintained supply route. Things were starting to look up.

We camped in a mission compound amongst some curious ducks and chickens and next to a grand red-brick cathedral with one remaining stained-glass window. We were welcomed for free by the priests who were interested in our journey. After collecting water from the well outside, Charlie and Chloe visited a nearby Médecins Sans Frontières clinic to say hello and have a look. Cheekily weighing themselves whilst chatting to the young doctor, they discovered that they had lost 15 lb each since leaving Kinshasa. I later found out I had lost over 22 lb. We managed to get in contact with the British officer in the UN base at Dungu (our next night's stop), but he had unexpectedly been called away to Bunia and had got stuck there due to the mounting storms. He gave us the name of a French officer whom he said would help us.

That evening and the next day's driving were uneventful. The roads were wide and made of compressed gravel, the only obstacles occasional car-deep holes filled with water. Sick of the delay caused by wading through them followed by sitting wet and muddy in the car—and annoyed at the lack of options to bypass them anyway—we stopped checking the depth. Inevitably we went through the deepest hole we'd encountered on the trip, with water washing over the bonnet and in through the air filters below the windscreen. Amazingly, 9Bob waded through, and our speed meant we didn't stall. We were experienced in these holes now. Within minutes, though, a grinding, whirring sound started to worry us. We quickly stopped and had a look but could not see anything wrong, and with only a few miles to go to Dungu we ploughed on.

Driving into Dungu was like arriving at an advertising convention for NGOs. All of the major well-known ones were there—Save the Children, World Vision, CARE, Refugee Council, etc.—as well as plenty that we had never heard of. Most affluent countries were represented on the signboards, from Denmark to Japan. Driving on the road that ran perpendicular to the main market street, every single house had an NGO sign outside. We later found out from UN staff that the NGOs liked to collocate with them for security reasons. The roads bustled with motorbikes and white Land Cruisers and were lined by children asking for biscuits. When we walked into shops (there were shops!) people asked us which NGO we were with.

Later we were to find out from several people in the UN that the LRA threat was exaggerated, and that every time the UN tried to downgrade the threat the NGOs lobbied to have it put back up because it enabled them to justify continued funding for their projects in Dungu. This also suited the UN personnel on the ground who received danger money (danger money!) for living in the UN bases in Dungu. We wished we had known the real story about the LRA earlier because it would have saved us a huge amount of worry. The whole thing was desperately cynical.

We pulled up outside the UN logistics base and asked for the French officer by name. He was a very kind man, and glancing at our grubby, dishevelled appearance, he asked us what we needed: a trained mechanic who could look at the rattling under the bonnet and a bed for the night. Both were completely against UN regulations but he sorted them both for us, firstly leading us to the mechanics. We arranged to come back in the morning to have a look at the car. Charlie in the meantime had discovered a company of Indonesian engineers in the adjacent camp. As he was Indonesian, and spoke Bahasa, we were invited to a cookery competition between the platoons the following night to celebrate *Iftar* near the end of Ramadan. It was undoubtedly the best food we'd had in the Congo.

It was a wonderfully relaxing evening sampling all the different foods and mixing with the Indonesians. They were based here to keep the road and bridges running from South Sudan and Uganda and they were a happy contingent, proud of the work that they were doing. They told us that Moke Bridge, the last bridge before South Sudan, had collapsed when an overloaded lorry had breached the weight limits, but they had built an emergency bridge which would hold us, so not to worry. They took it in turns to take their pictures with us.

The next morning we went over to the mechanics and met the legendary Jimmy, a Kenyan Land Rover-whisperer. Jimmy lent us a couple of mechanics and they helped us detach and clean the power steering pulley, hoping that was what was making the noise. While trying to move the vehicle we found the handbrake stuck on. 9Bob was starting to fall apart—surely he didn't want to stay in the Congo? Come on, just one more day! The mechanics graciously helped us again and took the handbrake apart and fixed it. By this point I was losing the will to live with all the work that I had had to do on 9Bob, and I could hardly stand to look at him. That said, considering his age, it was absolutely incredible what he had managed to do, and a testament to Land Rover's engineering.

When we finally got him moving again the grinding whirr was still audible. It was traced to the power steering pump, which had to be disconnected, consigning us to seven-point turns thereafter. While working on the car the mechanics also noticed a whole host of other issues: broken ball joints, a cracked internal bush on the front left radial arm (explaining a new clunk we'd noticed in Niangara) and a suspicious shock absorber. We had hoped to leave the next day, taking the opportunity to follow a security patrol heading in the same direction. They agreed to help fix 9Bob, but would not have time until the following day.

In the meantime we wandered over to the adjacent Guatemalan base, where their Special Forces had a fleet of very cool looking Land Rovers fitted with machine guns. We went to beg them for spare parts, particularly a bump stop, as the replacement Chloe had made with epoxy-glued layers of cut tyres had finally fallen off. We also needed a suspension coil. They were more than willing but unfortunately they had just arrived, and their spare parts had not yet caught up with them. Their pessimistic mechanic came to look at 9Bob and told us we would not make it out of the Congo without a new vehicle. They invited us to dinner instead, showed us their pet monkey and chameleons and listened to our story cobbled together in English, French and Spanish.

The next day we started early on 9Bob again, this time taking him out of the base to a deserted spot on the airfield because the mechanics were slightly worried that they would get caught helping us. Unfortunately, as we were leaving the base the DGM popped up, taking delight in seizing our passports. The day before the officials had come to us to ask for their usual pound of paperwork, but we had brushed them off in the hope that we could get away before we had to waste an hour or more with them. They were working here with the UN security and they would not let us off the base until we had registered. Even though we were just leaving to get the car fixed, and we would be back, what we should have done was to take the time to sit with them and fill in their paperwork.

Alas, it all got too much and I exploded at them, and at the UN security. Charlie and Chloe tried to restrain me but the pressure and the stress of the last two months made me see red. After nearly getting into a fight, we finally allowed them to look at our passports and, as they were convinced that we had delayed showing our documents to them because there was something wrong, they studied them closely. This drove me even madder as the mechanics were waiting for us outside the base.

By this point a crowd had gathered round, and the DGM proceeded to make the usual mistake of mixing up our Republic of Congo visas with our Democratic Republic of Congo visas. This was the final straw, and as Charlie and Chloe looked on in stunned silence, I proceeded to mock them in front of the crowd. Stupid. The DGM, desperate to get us for something, then pointed out that we only had four days left on our DRC visa and had missed the week deadline to renew the visas. We would have to pay a fine, either for overstaying or for renewing too late. It hadn't occurred to them that our location was within two days' drive of nearly three other countries, for one of which we had valid visas. This time it was Chloe's turn to lose her temper and shout that we were desperate to leave the Congo, if only to get away from inhospitable, greedy officials like the DGM. Stupid. We had won the (unnecessary) battle, but we had completely lost the war.

They let us go, and the mechanics fixed what they could on our vehicle, but when we got back to the base later that afternoon our friend the French officer told us that we had to leave and that we couldn't stay there another night. He didn't say it was because we (particularly me) had acted like children—he made up some bureaucratic excuse—but it was clear that that was the issue. He clearly had some sympathy for us because he said that he had rung the UN Inter Agency Camp in the centre of Dungu who had agreed to take us for the night—and nothing more. Even though the risk from the LRA was minimal, we still didn't want to take the risk and, it emerged, wouldn't be allowed to leave the town after nightfall anyway.

We drove down to the other base as the sun was setting and introduced ourselves to an Italian man whom we had been pointed towards. He sat us down and over supper listened to our story, tilting his head quizzically to one side every so often. 'Well,' he began, 'I have never, ever heard of a story like that. Are you completely and utterly mad?' Before we could respond he continued: 'You have, of course, heard what happened in South Sudan today?'

We hadn't, and so he proceeded to tell us: the president of South Sudan had just fired the vice president and the entire cabinet. The situation was very tense and violence between the two main ethnic groups (the president was Dinka, while most of those sacked were Nuer) looked like it was about to escalate. We quickly considered our other options: run to Central African Republic (falling apart), try to get to Uganda (long drive over some areas that were filled with rebels) or stay in the DRC. With little to choose from we opted to remain on course and head for South Sudan. The kind Italian smiled and shook our hands, wishing us luck. As he left he showed us the volleyball court where we were to camp—with any luck our last sleep in the Congo.

The next morning we got up well before light and completed our checks diligently on 9Bob. While it was still dark we nudged out of the UN base. To our left was a massive Belgian mock medieval *schloss* improbably standing with jungle creepers attempting to reclaim it. More bizarre, out-of-place, European architecture. It was raining. We had 136 miles to cover to the border. And we had to cover it in one day, not least because Charlie had realised the night before that if he didn't enter South Sudan today his South Sudanese visa would expire. We had stayed in the Congo a lot longer than we had expected to.

Thankfully, the road was good for the first ten miles. Gradually it deteriorated—maybe the people who had described it to us had not been beyond this point. Passing close to Garamba National Park we noticed some elephant dung in the road and several families of baboons, but didn't stop to look since the park was supposedly where the LRA hung out. The road was eerily quiet—we regretted missing the security of the convoy. The explanation for the lack of traffic became clear at Moke Bridge, however—an oversized lorry had tried to cross the emergency bridge the previous day (built because the original bridge had been destroyed by an oversized lorry), causing it to collapse into the river. Fortunately, as Charlie and I waded across the submerged wood beams and sandbags now forming a half-ford, Chloe was able to follow us, carefully getting 9Bob across without getting washed away by the rushing water.

We pushed through Faradje, avoiding the ubiquitous checkpoints because it was still pouring with rain. Finally we arrived in Aba, which despite being fifteen miles from the actual frontier had a locked gate across the road (much like the entry point eight weeks before). We pulled to a stop at about 3 pm— plenty of time, we thought, to get through and enter South Sudan.

We had to go around the different agencies, housed in beautiful, unmarked, empty colonial buildings, to get cleared for exit, an infuriatingly slow process. This was followed by a thorough search of our car—which attracted a large crowd. Tired of being exhibited and exploited, it was deeply frustrating when one of the myriad officials (all in t-shirts, jeans and sunglasses) tried to charge a fee to open the barrier on the border. Having crossed the whole Congo without paying a single bribe, we weren't about to start now, but the resulting argument was damaging, delaying us long enough for another bureaucrat to appear. Hilariously, for the first time in the Congo, the officials told Charlie off for taking photos and threatened to confiscate his camera. He was able to produce the photo permit that had taken us all day to get in Kinshasa!

Finally when we thought we had visited every agency possible, the Office Congolaise de Contrôle (OCC) popped up. It is unclear what its remit was, but the barely literate official took us to a dimly lit room with a desk where he proceeded to note down in an empty exercise book every visa in our passports for 'security reasons'—between us we must have had over one hundred visas.

Eventually they let us go and we drove across the barrier and floored it. The no-man's land between the DRC and South Sudan was about fifteen miles wide (as is quite common in Africa) and we raced across. One final search of our car and exit stamps, and finally we were out. In our haste we failed to get a photo of us under the border sign, which we all regret, but we were worried about not being let into South Sudan. We eventually made the South Sudan post at about 5 pm.

The Congo: 2,500 miles, sixty days, and not one bribe. We had made it.

***

South Sudan was marked by a string across the road. Eventually we persuaded the surly young soldiers to get up and let us in, and they escorted Charlie up the road to get permission from the immigration official to enter the village. Meanwhile the others, some of them stoned, milled around the car telling us in English, 'there is no problem here' and 'everything will be ok'. These stock phrases were repeated so many times over the next couple of hours that we began to be concerned.

The immigration official was a nice man called Edward, who apologised about all the formalities and was proud to welcome tourists to his new country. The village seemed to be an overflow from the army barracks in the centre, and we were guided up to it by the gaggle of soldiers, mainly unreformed militiamen with wide eyes. They were slightly surprised to see us and insisted on taking 9Bob apart and searching him. They were highly suspicious of Chloe's tampons, having never seen anything like it before, and were worried that Charlie's camera lens was a telescope, but we managed to convince them that we were not arms smugglers. A quiet crowd gathered to watch the spectacle, but not one person asked for a thing.

It then emerged that we could not actually legally enter South Sudan here—we would receive our stamps further on in a town called Yei. Major Moses, a towering hulk of a man, appeared and declared that there was no way that we could travel to Yei tonight—not now they had spent the last two hours of daylight searching the car. They blamed the danger posed by the LRA. Edward did, however, agree to mark us as entering South Sudan today so that Charlie's visa would still be valid. Once the car was searched, he offered us his office, which was a cosy mud hut just set back from the road, to sleep in. We agreed to meet at six am the next day. Edward had asked, and we had agreed, that we take Major Moses with us to Yei, where we were to get our entry stamps.

The next morning we were all ready to go at six, but there was no Edward and no army commander. We hung around for another hour, and still no-one had arrived. There were some militiamen standing around so we told them that we were going, at which they became quite agitated. Their English was not good enough to explain themselves so we got into 9Bob and drove off, fairly slowly, as the road was so bad. A couple of hundred yards further along we noticed that the militiamen were running after us and shouting, and then one of them jumped out of the bush in front of us with a rock in his hand aimed at the windscreen. I swerved the car and gunned the engine.

Slightly further down the road, with a cloud of shouting militiamen still following slowly moving 9Bob, we spotted Edward wandering along the road, clearly on his way to work. We pulled up beside him to thank him for his hospitality, and asked him to deal with the militiamen, telling him that we had waited around but no-one had come.

'Uh.'

That was the noise Charlie made as the muzzle of an AK47 was stuck into his neck by a wild, staring adolescent playing at being a soldier. The car was quickly surrounded as Edward was pushed out of the way. An angry soldier ran around the car hitting it with a stick, while more wild-eyed youths assembled with guns.

I switched off the car engine. Chloe sat very still in the middle seat, squinting at a second gun muzzle an inch from her nose. It was up to us to calm the situation down. I smiled a big smile and started talking soothing words. Out of the corner of my mouth, while staring directly at the youth most likely to kill Charlie, I told the others to smile and talk kindly and softly. We all put our hands out and open and began smiling at the adolescents pointing automatic weapons at us. Talking in a calm voice, I began agreeing with everything they said, saying anything really, just continuing to talk in a quiet, calm voice and all the while smiling and murmuring soothing words.

The kid with his weapon in Charlie's neck eventually removed it and we reversed the car slowly back to the barracks. The teenagers milled around us, alternatively pointing the weapons or not: it was madness. Imagine crossing the Congo and getting shot here.

We got back to the office and Charlie and I continued talking to the militiamen in quiet, calm voices. Meanwhile Chloe, who was being leered at, went and put on a long shawl (previously she had been wearing a t-shirt). We locked up 9Bob and stood next to it waiting for Edward to arrive. The youths shouted about breaking rules, which was odd because there didn't seem to be many rules there. They tried to demand the keys from us, but we made a deliberate act of putting them in pockets and saying that we wanted to speak with their officer and only he could demand our car keys. Gradually, talking to them calmly appeared to work, and the situation was defused. Edward arrived and left again, saying that he would go and get their officer.

While we waited the skies opened, thunder and lightning coming in close succession. Surely the road ahead, which they emphatically told us was awful, would only be worse now.

About ten minutes later we were invited into a hut with a row of seats on one side and a seat with a desk on the other. As we shuffled in, Edward appeared and sat apart from us at the side of the room. As we felt he was an ally of ours, we interpreted this as a slightly ominous sign. It was like being on trial. Eventually Major Moses walked in with an officer's cane and an impressive hat with gold braid. We all stood up.

After we had explained ourselves—and complained about having automatic weapons put in our faces by soldiers not wearing uniform—Moses spoke. He said he was sorry about the soldier in question and that things were tense at the moment with the situation in Juba (the capital). He understood that tourism was important to South Sudan and he recognised that this was not how to treat visitors. He would arrange to have that particular soldier flogged. Without pausing for our response he nodded to an aide, who distributed bottles of fizzy pop to us. Case closed!

'Now, can you take me to Yei,' he said, picking up a previously unnoticed, packed rucksack. We then realised that the whole sequence of events, including those actions that had nearly caused us mortal danger, had been arranged so that Moses could get a lift to town. Based on bitter experience from Afghanistan of the dangers of poor weapon discipline, I politely insisted that Moses showed me that his weapon was unloaded before allowing him to lever himself into the front seat. Chloe climbed into the boot and we set out along the moonscape of a road.

The remaining eighty miles to Juba were done over the next two days without event. The roads were terrible, and they tried to overcharge us for Charlie's visa (he had to buy a new one anyway) and then attempted to refuse our 2009 dollar bills because of a small smear of mud, but by now this was normal. The night before we reached Juba our stove finally ran out of gas; like so many things on the trip it had been very finely judged, completely by luck.

Postscript Chloe Baker

'Ça va un peu,' as the Congolese would say. Ok. Not that bad, not that good, but that's life. 'Ça va un peu' is the verbal equivalent of a shrug (Reybrouck 2014). It was probably the phrase that we heard the most in the Congo; it was the response to us asking how people were. The shrug conveys a sense of the fact that life is continuing, and there is not that much that the individual can do to shape it.

As we checked into a guest house on the banks of the Nile we surveyed ourselves. 'Ça va un peu.' That was about right. We had done it. But at that point it was too recent, too raw, too vivid to process. We felt like we had been subject to forces bigger than ourselves, that had affected us and that we couldn't control or understand. We arrived in Juba gaunt and wide-eyed and had to shake ourselves to adjust to the density and flow of people and traffic all around us. It had only been two months. We sat and played a lewd version of Scrabble in a bar overlooking the Nile, enjoying cold beers and pizza. Adding to our sense of incredulity, word spread in the hotel about our arrival and we found our table visited by expats keen to hear our story.

Writing this almost two years later, it still feels raw like an experience that will never dull, and we're still bewildered by all that we learnt. Besides the legendary corruption and violence in the DRC, there is kindness, generosity and a wicked sense of fun. There is also an immeasurable amount of suffering. We made light of the suffering at the time, sighing at the Congolese refrain 'nous souffrons'—the sigh perhaps a 'normal' reaction to having to process an uncomfortable mix of guilt, frustration, sympathy and despair—but in reality the Congolese people live lives that are simply not fair. We overcame seemingly insurmountable physical challenges, but the most difficult journey of all was navigating the complexities of this injustice, and of navigating the psychology and logics of Congolese society. This is where the Parable of the Scorpion and the Crocodile is helpful.

For Trefon the parable evokes self-destruction and equates extreme violence with social suicide—what he calls 'social cannibalism' (Trefon 2011). The predatory way we saw that the security forces and civil servants feed off the population certainly resonates with this idea. And what we perceived to be a lack of humanity was in reality a complete and unwavering lack of trust in anyone, or anything: an understandable 'every man for himself' mentality that is a product of multiple conflicts and appalling governments. The Congo has never had a good government. When a people is repeatedly betrayed, and then exploited, it becomes fatigued. The DRC is a country of normal human beings reacting to their own extraordinary life circumstances and events, the subjects (or objects?) of a terrible history. Dirty, exhausted, hungry and scared, we failed to grasp this and became ground down by people trying to get from us what they could, seeing us as an opportunity.

The parable also talks of misunderstanding. Trefon gives the example of the West investing in Joseph Kabila's government and thereby legitimising him, and continuing to provide development aid which is subverted, benefiting those in power who continue to abuse those they are meant to serve. Facts such as the assassination of Lumumba are often relegated to suspicion, belief and magic, while false rumours are accredited with the status of reality. These mistruths are cultivated and manipulated by those in power.

Because of this, the Congolese are very reluctant to express overt intention (to marry, to buy land, to move) for fear that the occult will interfere in plans before they are realised. This leads to a different relationship between what people say and what they do. Combined with pervasive secrecy at all levels of society, it is difficult for the uninitiated westerner to successfully navigate social interactions. What appeared glaringly obvious to us—a simple visual assessment of our physical reality, for example, being deeply entrenched in mud, clearly undernourished, exhausted and vulnerable—could be read and interpreted in a myriad of different ways by our Congolese observers, who interpret life through entirely different rules of causality. In Lomela, the more truth we told, the more incredulous our captors became.

But there is order amongst the disorder. As we saw, the Congolese 'carry within themselves the idea of a nation' which they value (Deibert 2013).

The resilience and resourcefulness of ordinary people was an inspiration, and could be the salvation of the country upon the cessation of outside interference. Positive changes may well come in the future as a result of small-scale, local social dynamism ('Trefon 2011), as we saw repeatedly on the road: people everywhere were still struggling to conquer their environment, working on the *sixième chantier* (sixth pillar).

What about us? We learnt a lot in the Congo, but we also lost a lot: not least the realisation that when you are pushed you sometimes act in ways of which you are ashamed. For all of our 'sophistication', we found ourselves to be base and weak. Mike and I were subjected to proper discrimination for the first time in our lives, with its incumbent stereotyping and objectification. It was an astonishingly powerful lesson, and reinforced our respect for people who rise above prejudice. Sadly, for Charlie the experience was nothing new—being mixed race, he had encountered prejudice all his life, and took less offence.

We learnt that in many ways our behaviour became irrelevant. Those around us had such fixed prejudices and expectations of us that what we said and did made no difference. The frustration and injustice of this weighed heavily on Mike and me. As our tempers became frayed with hunger and uncertainty, and we became impatient with people who were sometimes downright obstructive but sometimes just curious or confused, we began to behave in ways that we wouldn't at home. This really reinforced our fallibility as human beings, and we are not proud of how we conducted ourselves.

Yet sometimes the rawness was necessary: the middle of the Congo is a sink or swim kind of place. But we lost the ability to distinguish when bravado and threatened violence was necessary, and when it wasn't: when to get angry, when to bluff and when to shrug. We had got through, but we had lost our dignity, our composure, our 'civilisation'. This affected Mike the most, and Charlie and I often had to verbally restrain him, feeling ashamed at his disrespect and anger. I began to feel like I didn't know the man that I had been engaged to. Charlie was also affected: he failed to communicate honestly with his family and his girlfriend (now wife) about what he was doing, and worried them sick. As far as they were concerned, he was kidnapped or dead.

The personal journey was perhaps the most remarkable of all. Mike struggled with the guilt of ending our relationship. He also felt a weight of responsibility for our safety, particularly as we wouldn't have been in the Congo without his romanticism. As a result he behaved in ways I didn't know him capable of, and his actions took a toll on his health. He became very needy medically and for the only time in my career I struggled to willingly care for my patient, and to feel compassion amidst my own emotional turmoil.

I have never known such intense loneliness. To experience what felt like the end of the rest of my life, so far away from anyone I could share it with, is an experience I would not like to repeat. Fighting back the tears in internet cafés (when they were occasionally found) and reassuring my loved ones that all was well was for me the hardest thing of all. And this made me ashamed—that amongst so much suffering I could be so preoccupied with a broken heart.

So where did that leave us? The three of us had shared an experience that few would repeat. We had seen sides of each other that we would rather forget, as well as meeting plenty of people whom we warmly remember. We had also created something beautiful: the teamwork between us was real and strong. Right to the end, when one of us could see the other was coming to the end of their physical or emotional endurance, another would step forward and lead the discussion, coordinate the team or simply just take the machete and continue chopping trees.

There was no-one who would help us if we failed. Mike had to keep 9Bob running and keep us safe; I had to keep the three of us healthy; Charlie had to keep the path clear and keep our morale up, not to mention balancing his loyalty to Mike with fairness to me, which he did brilliantly. The fact that we had no choice but to be a team does not make it any less beautiful. It was made even more challenging by the fact that three-quarters of the journey was done in the hurt and anguish of the promise of shared life together breaking down. We lost many things in the Congo, but we will never forget the lessons we learnt there.

Shortly after arriving in Juba, Charlie and I flew home for work. Mike stayed behind in an uncertain, disintegrating Juba until he managed to sell 9Bob to an expat living there. Distributing, donating and dumping our remaining kit, he then got on a plane and flew home. The following year was spent putting our lives back together until finally the decision emerged to commit our experience to paper. Mike wrote the majority of *Crossing the Congo* from Myanmar, and Charlie assembled it in-between trips to Syria, Chad and Tanzania. I edited, researched and wrote from the Ebola Response in Sierra Leone.

Eighteen months after returning we all met for the first time in the National Café in Trafalgar Square. Amongst the memories and the laughter, there was a distant thought: where next?

Charlie, self-shot during foot operation

References

Butcher, Tim. 2009. *Blood River: The Terrifying Journey Through The World's Most Dangerous Country*. New York: Grove Press.

Calderisi, Robert. 2007. *The Trouble with Africa: Why Foreign Aid Isn't Working*. New York: St. Martin's Griffin.

Deibert, Michael. 2013. *The Democratic Republic of Congo: Between Hope and Despair*. London/New York: Zed Books.

Frankonia. 2012. 'Juba to Yaounde by Road'. *Thorntree Forum, Lonely Planet*. https://www.lonelyplanet.com/thorntree/forums/africa/topics/juba-to-yaounde-by-road-1294d723-5553-46bd-a425-3e92e64c0b9d.

Frederik and Josephine. 2010. 'Democratic Republic of Congo: Lubumbashi to Kinshasa - Expedition Portal'. http://www.expeditionportal.com/forum/threads/50799-Democratic-Republic-of-Congo-Lubumbashi-to-Kinshasa.

Harwood, Phil. 2013. *Canoeing the Congo: The First Source-to-Sea Descent of the Congo River*. Chichester: Summersdale.

Haynes. 2015. *Land Rover 90, 110 & Defender Diesel (83 - 07) up to 56*. https://haynes.co.uk/catalog/car-manuals/car-repair-manuals/land-rover/land-rover-90-110-defender-diesel-83-07-56.

ICRC and Ipsos. 2009. 'Democratic Republic of the Congo. Opinion Survey and In-Depth Research'. https://www.icrc.org/eng/assets/files/other/drc.pdf.

Moyo, Dambisa. 2010. *Dead Aid: Why Aid Is Not Working and How There Is Another Way for Africa*. London: Penguin.

RNDH. 2014. 'Rapport National sur le Développement Humain 2014 R.D. Du Congo | Human Development Reports'. http://hdr.undp.org/en/content/rapport-national-sur-le-d%C3%A9veloppement-humain-2014-rd-du-congo.

Rorison, Sean. 2012. *Congo*. Chalfont St Peter: Bradt.

Tarmo. 2011. 'Tarmo RTW: From South Sudan to DRC'. http://tarmo-rtw.blogspot.com/2011/07/from-south-sudan-to-drc.html.

Tayler, Jeffrey. 2001. *Facing the Congo: A Modern-Day Journey into the Heart of Darkness*. St. Paul, MN: Broadway Books.

Trefon, Theodore. 2011. *Congo Masquerade: The Political Culture of Aid Inefficiency and Reform Failure - African Arguments*. London: Zed Books.

Van Reybrouck, David. 2014. *Congo: The Epic History of a People*. London: Fourth Estate.